The Teacher in the Machine

The Teacher in the Machine

A HUMAN HISTORY
OF EDUCATION TECHNOLOGY

ANNE TRUMBORE

PRINCETON UNIVERSITY PRESS
PRINCETON & OXFORD

Copyright © 2025 by Princeton University Press

Princeton University Press is committed to the protection of copyright and the intellectual property our authors entrust to us. Copyright promotes the progress and integrity of knowledge created by humans. Thank you for supporting free speech and the global exchange of ideas by purchasing an authorized edition of this book. If you wish to reproduce or distribute any part of it in any form, please obtain permission.

Requests for permission to reproduce material from this work should be sent to permissions@press.princeton.edu

Published by Princeton University Press
41 William Street, Princeton, New Jersey 08540
99 Banbury Road, Oxford OX2 6JX

press.princeton.edu

GPSR Authorized Representative: Easy Access System Europe - Mustamäe tee 50, 10621 Tallinn, Estonia, gpsr.requests@easproject.com

All Rights Reserved

Library of Congress Cataloging-in-Publication Data
Names: Trumbore, Anne M., 1966– author.
Title: The teacher in the machine : a human history of education technology / Anne M. Trumbore.
Description: Princeton, New Jersey : Princeton University Press, 2025. | Includes bibliographical references and index.
Identifiers: LCCN 2024058057 (print) | LCCN 2024058058 (ebook) | ISBN 9780691198767 (hardback) | ISBN 9780691237619 (ebook)
Subjects: LCSH: Educational technology—History—United States. | Education, Higher—Effect of technological innovations on—United States. | Artificial intelligence—Educational applications—United States. | BISAC: EDUCATION / Computers & Technology | EDUCATION / Distance, Open & Online Education
Classification: LCC LB1028.3 .T75 2025 (print) | LCC LB1028.3 (ebook) | DDC 371.33/4—dc23/eng/20240108
LC record available at https://lccn.loc.gov/2024058057
LC ebook record available at https://lccn.loc.gov/2024058058

British Library Cataloging-in-Publication Data is available

Editorial: Matt Rohal and Alena Chekanov
Production Editorial: Nathan Carr
Jacket/Cover Design: Katie Osborne
Production: Erin Suydam
Publicity: Tyler Hubbert, Alyssa Sanford, and Kathryn Stevens

Jacket/Cover Credit: PLATO Terminal with Mathematical Problem. 1960. Teaching Machine developed in Coordinated Science Laboratory under Prof. Don Bitzer. Image #0001140 courtesy of the University of Illinois Archives.

This book has been composed in Arno

Printed in the United States of America

10 9 8 7 6 5 4 3 2 1

To all the humans in the loop who wrote the code,
designed the courses, taught the classes, created the
business plans, conducted the research, fixed the bugs,
and never got rich.

CONTENTS

Introduction: A Human in the Loop   1

Part I. The Education-Industrial Complex   13

1   The Men behind the Curtain   15

     East Palo Alto, California   15

     The Thrill of (Re)Discovery   17

     Teaching Machines   21

     Education in a Box   23

     The Business of Teaching Machines   24

     Bad Things Happen in Philadelphia   26

     Balls in the Air   29

     Government Funding in Edtech   31

     The QWERTY Theory of Educational Technology   34

2   Experimenting for the Future   37

     From Teaching Machines to Machine Learning   37

     Seymour Papert Asks, "Who's the Boss?"   40

     Suppes Dreams of a Tutor for Every Child   42

		PLATO Connects Learners	47
		The Education-Industrial Complex	53
	3	Commercialization	57
		Using Technology to Connect to Industry: Stanford Instructional Television Network	61
		Using Technology to Expand Influence: The Computer Curriculum Corporation	61
		Using Technology to Transmit Democracy: The Nicaragua Radio Mathematics Project	65
		Using Technology to Make Money: PLATO IV	67
		Using Educational Technology as a Tool for Learning	73
		Using Technology to Disrupt	77
		Using Technology to Change the World: One Laptop per Child	78
		Using Technology to Expand Access	81
		Stanford Online High School	83
		Putting the Tech in Edtech	86

Part II. The Business of Higher Education			87
	4	Learning Gets Managed and Monetized	93
		Spreading the Higher Education Gospel on the Internet	93
		Managing Learning	97
		1994: U.S. Office of Educational Technology	99
		Another Gold Rush	100

	Fathom	101
	All Learn	102
	Why MIT Decided to Give Away All Its Course Materials via the Internet	104
	Open Learning Initiative: Carnegie Mellon Marries Research and Practice	106
	OER and Open University	107
	Pricing Universities Out of Business	109
	Working on the Farm	110
5	MOOCs, 2012	113
	July 2012, Mountain View, California, 11:30 a.m.	113
	Follow the Code	115
	The Office of Technology Licensing	117
	Clash of the Titans	120
	The Invisible Hand	123
	Founding Father	126
	Surfing the Tsunami	128
	When in Doubt, Optimize	135
	Different Time Zone, Different Business Model	136
6	Riding the Waves	139
	The Great Unbundling	145
	The Golden Loophole	149
	"Let's Wash This Money through the Laundromat"	150

	Is This What We Meant by Globalization?	156
	OPMs Zig, Coursera Zags	158
7	Covid, Cash-Outs, and ChatGPT	165
	Cashing In and Out	169
	The Learner Can Be a Winner	173
	Only a Fool Would Make Predictions, Especially about the Future	176
	"History Will Teach Us Nothing"?	179
	Conclusion	183
	Coming Apart at the Polysemes	183
	The Violence of Forgetting	189

Acknowledgments	193
How I Wrote This Book: Notes on Sources	195
Notes	201
Index	223

Introduction

A Human in the Loop

> Machines are worshipped because they are beautiful, and valued because they confer power; they are hated because they are hideous, and loathed because they impose slavery.
>
> —BERTRAND RUSSELL

> I like the dreams of the future better than the history of the past.
>
> —THOMAS JEFFERSON

> I am not sure exactly which applications will be profitable. But you never bet against technology.
>
> —YOUNG VENTURE CAPITALIST AT A BLOCKCHAIN CONFERENCE

Since the middle of the twentieth century, professors, administrators, and staff at some of the United States' most prestigious universities have been creating educational technology that has changed the way we experience and think about college education. At the same time, cogent arguments have been made that disruption from educational technology is a potent myth[1] perpetuated by elite scientists who assume they can use science and technology to improve education.[2] It is certainly true that belief in these ideas of disruption in 2025, accelerated by the financial incentives for standardization and scaling of education, guides those who are inventing these new technologies to perpetuate a traditional style of education (e.g., listening to lectures, reading, taking tests) that favors the wealthy, Western, and already educated.[3] Digging deeper, these technologies first benefit a remarkably homogeneous group of venture capitalists, technology executives, and university administrators before they help students. This is by design: the Silicon Valley playbook calls for "keeping the networks tight and personal" to tilt the odds in favor of success. As historian Margaret O'Mara writes, "The business of entrepreneurship and VC took place not only in boardrooms and cubicles but over beers and peanuts ... late-night coding sessions and poker games, on forty-mile bicycle rides. . . . It was a wonderful world if you were in it, and a tough place to hack into if you didn't have the time, the money, the poker skills, or the $10,000 bike."[4] Today, the elite universities that created and profit from these technologies educate the overwhelming majority of the venture capitalists and tech executives who fund and run them.

Yet there is a deeper history of these uses of educational technology, a history that predicted AI-enabled tutoring, online learning communities, and the power of teaching children to use technology as a tool to build their own knowledge. In the 1960s three institutions—Stanford, MIT, and the University of Illinois—backed significant experiments in using computers in education. Patrick Suppes at Stanford pursued a vision of the computer as an "individual Aristotle," the intellectual progenitor of intelligent tutors and instructional chatbots. Seymour Papert at MIT, an inaugural codirector (with Marvin Minsky) of the Artificial Intelligence Lab (now CSAIL), created a programming language for children so that they might use computers as a tool. And Don Bitzer, of the University of Illinois, created PLATO, a networked course distribution system that educated up to a thousand learners at once, featuring touch-screen technology, plasma displays, and real-time communication with other users (in 1972!). Each of these experiments was revolutionary for its time, decades before the "financialization of higher education" that began in the 1990s[5] concurrent with the rise of for-profit universities as a means of saddling learners with student loan debt for the enrichment of investors.[6]

We are now in a moment when these older experiments can have greater resonance. The Covid-19 pandemic revealed the limits and the benefits of online education, generative AI has the capabilities to fulfill Suppes's vision of "individual Aristotles" providing individualized tutoring at scale, and the justifiability of higher education is at an all-time low. The power of generative AI alone should have us revisit Papert's vision that *"the child programs the computer,* and, in doing so, ... acquires a sense of mastery over a piece of the most modern and powerful technology."[7] The ideas and practices of the earliest days of online education can be a valuable resource for designing its future and resisting the forces of financialization if those who are creating it understand the political, financial, and personal stories that have brought the field to where it is today.

Sociologists use the term "educational entrepreneurs" to define academic leaders who pursue the expansion of the funding, influence, and function of their universities and whose efforts have been responsible for the massive growth of higher education in the United States. Alexander Kindel and Mitchell Stevens have expanded the concept of "educational entrepreneurship" to mean time periods when "academic credentials can be made (into) viable solutions to social problems."[8] Adopting this framework, this book examines two periods of educational entrepreneurship, one in the 1960s and 1970s and a second beginning in 2012. Each of these periods was partially defined by the technology that enabled it: the computer, or hardware, used as an educational tool in the 1960s and the internet and software of the 2010s that allowed first for the broad dissemination of online courses and then, shortly after, rapid assimilation of artificial intelligence into the classroom. Each of these technologies conferred power on those who were able to finance it, giving them control over how it was developed and implemented. The first part of this book reveals the history of the use of computers in education as an instrument of government authority during the Cold War, a time when many believed that education was a public good that would enable a thriving society and ensure U.S. power internationally. The second part focuses on the development of online education as a tool for universities and investors to generate revenue and expand their influence during a time when higher education was seen, increasingly, as a private investment. The differences in the social and historical contexts of these periods, and what educational entrepreneurship means in each era, reveal a set of considerations any student, parent, school, or university must keep in mind when developing and using technology to improve and extend education.

My own career has spanned both of these periods. I was hired by Pat Suppes in 2004 to work on a web-based grammar program that gave students feedback on their responses. My role was quite literally to be the "human in the loop," creating an adaptive learning experience by pushing prewritten feedback and next-question pathways in response to their work. (This software is still available, in a much-augmented form, through McGraw-Hill.)[9] As access to broadband internet expanded, our next big project was to create the Stanford Online High School,[10] which predated "Zoom School" by fourteen years. Then, in early 2012, I was hired by Andrew Ng at his new start-up, Coursera, as the mania about Massive Open Online Courses

(MOOCs) was gripping higher education. And since 2015, I have worked at the University of Pennsylvania and the University of Virginia to lead efforts to create online certificates and degrees in topics valued by industry (e.g., data science, business administration, computing, and information technology). In short, I have been an ensemble player in the transformation of online education from experimental and low status to "innovative" and "disruptive." I have also helped make wealthy institutions, venture capitalists, and more than a few professors even wealthier.

In fact, the questions that would animate the idea for this book began in the summer of 2012, when I was standing in a cramped office with a soul-sucking gray carpet at Coursera, trying not to weep at the endless flood of emails from professors at Princeton and the University of Michigan with whom I was creating their very first MOOCs. Online education wasn't new; it had been offered for decades, most publicly by the for-profit University of Phoenix. And its roots went back even further: the head of my group at Stanford, Professor Patrick Suppes, had helped establish the field of computer-assisted instruction before I was born.[11] Yet, the designs and technologies developed over the previous fifty years now were being "invented" by leading computer scientists in artificial intelligence, financed by prestigious venture capital firms, and used to offer open enrollment courses by universities that had built their reputations over hundreds of years by the high quality of students they could exclude. It seemed as though everyone had willfully forgotten all the work that had come before.

Although I spent a great deal of my time at Coursera feeling underwater, I wasn't naive enough to think that the preeminent financiers and higher education institutions backing and working with the company were investing all this time and money to give education away for free. There had to be another angle. The most obvious motive was profit, but Coursera did not have a paywall. And the initial partner institutions (Princeton, Stanford, the University of Michigan, and the University of Pennsylvania) had newsworthy endowment wealth, so it was unlikely that they "needed" any money they might eventually make from MOOCs. And money didn't explain why no one was acknowledging the history and scholarship of the field in any meaningful way. After researching the social and historical contexts for this book, I believe the history of online education was deliberately ignored for three main reasons: innovation drives adoption (no one wants to invest in an "old" idea), venture capital profits from scale and standardization (which can leave individualization behind), and the idea of using technology to make education both more efficient and democratic consolidates power in the hands of the "disrupters" who are almost always businessmen and scientists educated at the most elite universities in the world.

The force of forgetting in educational technology should not be underestimated. One need look no further than Sal Khan, who seemingly can't help reinventing education (and announcing it in a TED Talk). In 2011, the popularity of his talk, "Let's Use Video to Reinvent Education,"[12] inspired the first highly publicized MOOCs and ignited interest in venture capital investment in educational technologies.[13] Kahn's promises about the ability of video to disrupt how people learn[14] were inspiring, so long as you were totally unaware of the ongoing experiments in computer-assisted math instruction that had been conducted over the previous decades.[15] Which, to be fair, the philanthropists and corporations that bankrolled Khan Academy probably were.

Never one to let a new technology go to waste in the service of transforming education, Khan returned to TED in April 2023 to claim, "We're at the cusp of using AI for probably the biggest positive transformation that education has ever seen. And the way we are going to do that is by giving every student on the planet an artificially intelligent but amazing personal tutor."[16] Khan gave little evidence beyond the anecdotal that an artificially intelligent tutor would be effective, nor did he address any reasonable downsides of giving an "amazing" personal chatbot to every student, including (but not limited to) devaluing teacher expertise and relationships with students, placing additional demands on teachers to understand and deploy the new technology, restricting the definition of "learning," and increasing bias and discrimination in classrooms and schools.[17]

He also did not mention (at least) three important facts.

1. Khanmigo, the amazing personal tutor, couldn't do math.[18]
2. The two-sigma effect he cited about the transformative effects of tutoring, authored by Benjamin Bloom in 1984, has been replicated only once in forty years.[19]
3. Education had already seen the power of giving students an artificially intelligent personal tutor; in fact, one widely publicized demonstration took place less than five miles away from Khan's elementary lab school.

Khan's influence on the use of technology in education is significant, and the products he is providing to students and schools systems are helpful to many. Additionally, Khan never incorporated and kept his business a nonprofit (although he draws a salary of over a million dollars a year).[20] He is clearly passionate about education, a phrase I have heard not only from Khan but from almost every edtech leader (including the founders of edX, Coursera, Emeritus, and many of their senior staff). But why does having a passion for education and an MBA/PhD from Stanford/Harvard/MIT (or equivalent) qualify one to "disrupt" education in the first place?

There is a long history of scholarship on educational technology that rightly questions its ability to make much of a difference in addressing the educational problems of access, engagement, and relevance it seeks to solve. Currently, scholars like Larry Cuban, Roy Pea, Justin Reich, Audrey Watters, Ken Koedinger, Ryan Baker, and George Siemens, among many others, have sought to discover what technologies work in education and for whom they provide the most benefits. But universities generally don't use evidence-based research when selecting educational technology and they "buy as a pack" (i.e., do what everyone else is doing), behaviors edtech companies exploit to their own advantage. Universities also appoint innovation experts who look a lot like edtech founders and funders, which mutes questions about why venture capital and private equity find technological solutions to the educational attainment struggles of minorities, working adults, and veterans worthy of investment.

In the earliest days of computer-assisted instruction, the inventors of these technologies conducted scholarly studies themselves. Supported by their universities and government grants, and mindful of their reputations as scholars, they were not primarily motivated by profit. In this mid-twentieth century period of educational entrepreneurship, universities wanted to increase their influence and prestige and generate revenue to support faculty, curriculum, and students. In the second period of educational entrepreneurship, in the early part of this century, university professors and graduate students left the university to seek funding from venture capital, private equity, and, in Khan's case, philanthropy, where "sustainability" and "scalability" (codes for profitability) are the main motives for investment. And while universities' aims today may be similar to those they held in the past, they are far more beholden to the market than in the previous century, when they essentially owned the technologies that were produced on their campuses.

One can compare two uses of technology in these two different eras at Stanford to see the contrast in historical context. In 1969, Stanford developed the Stanford Instructional Television Network (SITN), primarily to address the logistical challenges of transporting employed engineering students to and from Stanford's Palo Alto campus during weekdays, when they were working. By solving the logistical challenges of extending educational offerings to a new population of working learners, Stanford strengthened its connections to local technology firms and expanded its instructional reach. However, SITN was part of a more ambitious strategy to both increase the university's influence and prestige and generate revenue intended to support the expansion of the faculty, broaden the curriculum, and benefit both on-campus and off-campus students.

In 2011, this same strategy supported several Stanford professors in offering the first Massive Open Online Courses (MOOCs) to capture the public imagination. Although Stanford's aims in facilitating these initial courses were nearly identical to those for SITN, the execution of each initiative could not have been more different. While SITN was primarily homegrown—meaning the technology and designs for the program were created and controlled by the university—MOOCs were led by individual professors and financed by private capital; ultimately, the attention they received would spur hundreds of millions of dollars in investment and result in the formation of three companies whose evolving business models would begin to crack open the purpose of the university and the value of an undergraduate degree.

The differences in these two experiments reveal a significant shift in the public perception of college: from a public good supported by the government through federal and state funding to a private investment in an individual financed through private loans. As education scholar Paul Tough said, "Over the last few decades, we've quietly changed our system from one that allowed people from working class backgrounds to get a reasonably priced education that would improve their opportunities, to a system with dramatically reduced public funding that puts the financial burden on individual students and their families."[21] But it is the similarities between these two periods that show us why online education has had such a destabilizing effect on the traditional business of education.

First, both periods rely on the belief that education is in crisis. The details of these crises may differ across decades, but the claim that education is in need of reform has been consistent for over a century. Second, many of the proposed educational reforms assume that education should be more efficient—in both costs and effectiveness. Third, technology is a perennial solution to creating higher-quality, lower-priced educational experiences that are available to a greater number of learners. And finally, technological disruptors are uniquely qualified to solve these problems by virtue of being able to sell the need for disruption to funders and buyers of the technologies, despite having little experience in trying to educate students (although they have generally done quite well at being educated, since most of them have multiple degrees from elite institutions).

At the same time, universities should be cautious about dismissing educational technologies, if only for the reason that if universities dismiss them, they will lose influence over how these technologies are developed and deployed. Both online education and generative AI's uses in education will expand in the coming decades. My hope is that by knowing the origins of online education and its relationship with artificial intelligence, as well as its trajectory to the present, universities can be more clear-eyed about their business partnerships with technology companies, more thoughtful about their motives in distributing education "to the masses," and ultimately take inspiration from the past's successes and failures in order to create more equitable educational experiences that provide more returns to learners than edtech investors.

PART I
The Education-Industrial Complex

1

The Men behind the Curtain

East Palo Alto, California

The cameras were rolling. It was a good day for a shoot, and so far, both the weather and the humans were cooperating. The children at Brentwood Elementary School filed into their classroom like professional actors. Almost no one looked at the cameraman as they sat down and took their seats in front of their individual computer screens. Quietly, they put on their headphones and waited for the screens to light up.

Showtime. Now, all that had to happen was for the damn thing to work. The professor was coolly confident, but the grad student couldn't stop his hands from shaking. They were about to do what had never been done before: to use the latest technology and advances in artificial intelligence to provide each student with an automatic tutor—a computerized companion who would respond to each child at their own level and help them learn at their own pace. And while the vision was grand, the tools they had to work with were not. The research team had worked around the constraints by combining different electronic components—processors, audio, recording devices, screens, and specialized "pencils"—to create a system of hardware that could support their instructional software. The professor and his colleagues had convinced the Department of Education to give the research group a sizable grant to run this experiment. Now the press had gotten wind of it and wanted to see how it worked.

In a room behind the classroom, the graduate student stood in front of the IBM processor, double-checking that the audio files were synced to the correct visuals and that the disk for recording the students work was working. With sixteen students on the system at the same time, and the cameras rolling, there was no room for error. Without being able to see the students, all the grad student could do was wait, and hope the system performed as the research team had built it to.

The cameraman zoomed in on the screen from behind a young girl's shoulder. The pearlized buttons on the back of her dress glinted in the light. "Look at the picture and the word," said the computer, showing an illustration of a ham, and the letters H A M. "The word is ham. . . . Touch and say ham." The young girl with cropped black hair looked at a list of words on the screen. Slowly, she reached for the word "ham." She touched it and said, "Ham." "Yes," said the computer, "Ham."

Success. The grad student exhaled. His professor, who had been watching the students in the classroom, spoke directly to the camera. "The learning becomes more efficient," he said. "The teacher will be free to work individually with children having learning difficulties."

The reporter could not contain his excitement even in the closing shot. With the students playing at recess behind him, he looked directly into the camera and spoke. "We now have the tools to take a giant step and extend the frontiers of education into the future."[1]

A new era of education was about to begin: one where any student who wanted an education could get one quickly and inexpensively. In this era, students would not face geographic or financial barriers to quality instruction. Not only would education be delivered directly to learners but it would also be personalized, using artificial intelligence, so the student could learn more quickly and deeply than in the traditional classroom. Powered by the rapidly accelerating capabilities of technology and artificial intelligence, this new era would raise the level of education across the globe to respond to the new demands of a rapidly changing economy. It was an exciting time of promise and new advances.

It was also 1966.

The Thrill of (Re)Discovery

We make the same discoveries about online education decade after decade because we do not acknowledge—or know—the history of the field. There is evidence that this ignorance is not an accident.[2] Estimates have the educational technology market projected to be valued at $549.6 billion in 2033,[3] and the main driver of its adoption is innovation: the idea that the technology and its possibilities are brand-new.

Yet the history of educational technology is over one hundred years old. And the use of computers in education, which made online education possible, has a birthdate in the middle of the twentieth century. On September 2, 1958, President Dwight D. Eisenhower signed the National Defense Education

Act (NDEA) in reaction to the successful launch and orbit of the Soviet satellite *Sputnik*.[4] Designed to promote a more technologically skilled and educated population, the NDEA established federal funding for education in the form of both student loans and expanding education in science, mathematics, and foreign languages—all subjects highly in demand during the Cold War. The NDEA also put new focus on the need to provide quality instruction to larger numbers of students quickly. Using technology to personalize learning was a priority for research at the time, as it is today, because it "encompasses in its language, aspirations and implementation earlier progressive reforms in the early twentieth century, the 1960's, the 1990's and the present."[5]

At the same time, early experiments in artificial intelligence were exploring how a machine could learn and interact with humans. Then in 1962, the Advanced Research Projects Agency (ARPA) "radically changed the scale of research in AI, propelling it from a collection of small projects into a large-scale, high-profile domain."[6] By the early 1960s, education was a national imperative, artificial intelligence was a rapidly growing field, and academics were eager to explore how the computer could be used to personalize learning at scale.

Although many universities experimented with educational technology, three professors led initiatives at Stanford, the University of Illinois, and MIT that shaped the conversations we are having today about artificial intelligence and education. Their experiments would help establish the field of online education as they grappled with ways to expand access to education while improving its adaptability to learners of different abilities. Their attempts to bring their inventions to market reveal the changing roles of the university from government-funded research centers to entrepreneurial businesses. Their historical context puts in sharp relief the shift from higher education as a public good to a private investment in an individual. And their stories show the interconnectedness of higher education, technology, government, and the marketplace.

Patrick Suppes, a professor of philosophy at Stanford University, established the Computer-Based Learning and Teaching Laboratory in 1962 with a $1 million grant from the Carnegie Corporation (about $10 million in 2023). Widely known as the "father" of computer-assisted instruction, Suppes worked for the next fifty years exploring the uses of computers in education. His experiments were the first educational programs that truly "scaled" across geographic boundaries, using the telephone, radio, and ultimately the internet to meet students where they were—at home, or in their local schools, all across the world. A compatriot of John McCarthy, himself a father of artificial intelligence, Suppes was also an early pioneer of individualized instruction and dreamed of the computer as an "individual Aristotle" that would offer personalized tutoring to learners everywhere.

Donald Bitzer, a professor of electrical engineering at the University of Illinois, oversaw the development of the most sophisticated educational system of the 1960s, 1970s, and 1980s: PLATO. A distributed computer-based learning system, PLATO could support up to one thousand students around the world doing coursework, playing early versions of video games, and chatting with their friends on message boards simultaneously. "All of the features you see kids using now, like discussion boards or forums and blogs, started with PLATO," Bitzer said in 2020. "All of the social networking we take for granted actually started as an educational tool."[7]

Seymour Papert, professor of applied mathematics and education at MIT, held a revolutionary and contrarian view of computers in education. He believed that children should program computers and not the other way around. Working closely with the other "father" of artificial intelligence, Marvin Minsky, Papert thought deeply about how humans learned as a framework for how machines could learn. His seminal artificial intelligence work, *Perceptrons*, coauthored by Minsky, introduced the idea of neural networks, while his groundbreaking education work, *Mindstorms*, argued for the importance of teaching computer languages to young children to encourage them to use computers as a tool. He created the first computer programming language, Logo, included on early personal computers, that empowered children to program. Papert also inspired the One Laptop per Child initiative, which delivered millions of laptops to children around the world. His ideas continue to power the maker movement, project-based learning, and easy-to-use computer languages like Scratch that enable children to create apps and programs.

The visions of these three men are still instantiated today in almost every major technology deployed for education, from hardware like touch screens, laptops, plasma displays, and toy robots, to software like advanced chatbots (e.g., Google's Bard and ChatGPT), to adaptive instructional programs and educational games and apps like DuoLingo and Quizlet, to online courses distributed from Coursera and edX. Yet their history is obscured by the constant onslaught of the new, particularly new inventions that claim to solve "new" educational problems. But just beneath the shiny surface of the latest edtech marvel is the work of Suppes, Bitzer, and Papert and the many people on their teams who have worked, sometimes unknowingly, to extend the past of educational technology into the future. While their stories show the promise of using technology to improve education, they also illustrate the perils of forgetting its history, including rushing products into the market, making business decisions that privilege the market over the learner, designing products and programs for traditionally successful students, creating an edtech innovation ecosystem whose members—from product designers to entrepreneurs to venture capitalists—are astonishingly nondiverse, and ultimately leaving the most vulnerable learners behind. Perhaps by bringing their history to light we can chart the progress of educational technology more clearly and see a pathway to a future even brighter than what the early pioneers imagined.

Teaching Machines

> There are more people in the world than ever before, and a far greater part of them want an education. The demand cannot be met simply by building more schools and training more teachers. Education must become more efficient.
>
> —B. F. SKINNER, *SCIENCE*, 1958

The efforts to integrate technology into education did not begin with computers. In January 1929, Sidney Pressey signed an agreement with W. M. Welch Manufacturing (a company that sold furniture and laboratory supplies to schools and hospitals) to build an "Automatic Teacher" to combat "educational drudgery and incompetence."[8] The notion that automation was capable of improving teaching quality was rooted in the assumption that teachers themselves were not effective, which arose with the "feminization" of teaching in the United States in the 1800s.[9] Yet, the Automatic Teacher wasn't a teacher at all—it didn't deliver lessons or educational content. Instead, it was an Automatic Tester, giving individualized feedback to student answers on assessments. In fact, the positive reaction to the machine was due to its purported ability to personalize feedback and do it for more students than a human: a goal every subsequent technology, from computers to online instruction to ChatGPT, claims to make possible. Additionally, Pressey's idea of the student using the machine to direct his or her own learning was further developed and strengthened by Seymour Papert at MIT when he created a computer language expressly for children to direct the computer to help them learn.

Pressey was ahead of his time in two meaningful ways: (1) the technology available to him wasn't powerful enough to fully implement his vision, and (2) theories of education as a behavior were not yet developed or accepted enough to provide fertile ground for the idea of practice, assessment, or learning by doing to be seen as valuable.[10] When the Automatic Teacher was advertised in the spring of 1929, Pressey received congratulations for his work and interest in his product from his peers at multiple institutions, including Stanford. But by the time the machine was ready to ship, the stock market had crashed, and the country was entering the Great Depression. Suddenly, there was a surplus of human labor, and the idea of automating instruction fell out of favor. Pressey's machine was discontinued in 1933 due to lack of sales.[11] But while Pressey's machine was not marketable, his vision for improving efficiency and quality in education continues to be taken up today. Two decades after Pressey's Automatic Teacher, another professor, this one at Harvard, would popularize Pressey's ideas, initially claiming that he had no knowledge of Pressey's work. Even in the 1950s, educational technology was in the process of forgetting itself.

Education in a Box

B. F. Skinner rose to notoriety for supposedly raising his younger daughter in a box. In 1945, he wrote an article for *Ladies' Home Journal* about his invention of an "air crib," which was part temperature-controlled elevated playpen and part crib. The idea was to create a labor-saving device for child-rearing, but public imagination (and the article) conflated the "air crib" with the Skinner box, a device for observing animal behavior and conducting research experiments. The article, titled "Baby in a Box," helped make the connection between animal experimentation and human experiments and drew a firestorm of attention.[12] (Claims of child cruelty were wildly overstated and his daughter was unharmed by her time in the air crib.) Undeterred by the national attention, Skinner kept teaching, and experimenting, developing his theory of behaviorism while advising a cadre of graduate students who would rise to prominence in psychology.[13] And then, in 1953, he walked into his older daughter's grade school classroom and left "horrified" by the inefficiency he saw there. "In light of our present knowledge, a school system must be called a failure if it cannot induce students to learn except by threatening them for not learning," he would later write.[14] Skinner had an idea for a new kind of box: one that would teach. That night he went home and built a prototype for his first teaching machine.

Skinner would spend most of the next decade trying to find a business partner to help develop and build his teaching machine to no avail. Although he worked with several well-known companies (including IBM, Rheem Manufacturing, and Harcourt Brace and Jovanovich), he could never get his machines mass-produced despite countless hours of work on the partnerships. Skinner was far more successful as a public intellectual who popularized the idea of automated instruction. And while he initially ignored Pressey as an early inventor of teaching machines, he gave him (begrudging) credit in his widely read 1958 article for *Science*, "Teaching Machines": "Nevertheless, Pressey seems to have been the first to emphasize the importance of immediate feedback in education and to propose a system in which each student could move at his own pace. He saw the need for capital equipment in realizing these objectives. Above all he conceived of a machine which (in contrast with the audio-visual aids which were beginning to be developed) permitted the student to play an active role."[15] And although Skinner's attempts to commercialize his ideas failed, one company was successful in bringing them to market.

The Business of Teaching Machines

IBM had a long-held interest in teaching machines. Starting with the typewriter, which was shown to improve learning outcomes when used in the classroom, and then moving to machines that automated the grading, or scoring, of tests, IBM approached Skinner in 1954 with interest in developing a "teaching box" that would automate instruction that IBM could mass-produce. But after several years of bureaucratic foot-dragging, and stringing Skinner along through the development of several prototypes that were never mass-produced, IBM decided to forgo producing Skinner's teaching machine and reassigned his patents back to him.[16]

Meanwhile IBM continued to focus on the development of the 650, an early computer, which the company felt could teach basic math. The debut of the plans for the program for basic math instruction run on an IBM 650 marked a huge leap forward in the conception of teaching machines. For the first time, the machine

FIGURE 1. Student at an IBM 650, ca. 1960. The IBM 650, and the culture that spawned it, fundamentally altered commerce, science, and higher education. From the IBM Archives, https://www.ibm.com/history/650.

itself did not have to be manufactured; instead a software program, which could be easily modified at minimal expense, could be sold to run on an existing machine. The flexibility and comparatively low cost of developing computer programs versus manufacturing teaching machines meant that a new set of scientists would take up the challenges of both standardizing and individualizing instruction: computer scientists.[17]

IBM made sure it was getting the best minds in the country thinking about how to advance its products. The company would "grant" universities IBM computers at reduced rates in exchange for the university's computer scientists keeping IBM informed about how they were using the machines and what improvements they felt the company should make to advance their research. "The program of educational grants for universities who were teaching either business school courses or a set of courses in the liberal arts colleges on computing where you'd get up to sixty percent rental reductions. That was a program that I started, I guess, in 1955. That became very widespread,"[18] recalled Cuthbert Hurd, who founded the applied science department at IBM (and hired famed mathematician John von Neumann). Today, we recognize this model as "beta testing" or "soft launch" where customers are given free access to a product or service in return for their feedback. This practice further brought down the high cost of computing time and allowed professors to experiment, research, and "dream big" about the capabilities for the computer. Yet, it was a group from IBM, not a university, who would create the initial blueprint for educational software.

Bad Things Happen in Philadelphia

In 1958, the University of Pennsylvania and the Air Force Office of Scientific Research hosted "The Conference on the Art and Science of the Automatic Teaching of Verbal and Symbolic Skills" in Philadelphia. In a foreword to the published conference proceedings, Eugene Galanter, a professor of mathematical psychology at the University of Pennsylvania, wrote, "The general form that the arguments take is that the machines are merely aids to teaching." But Galanter, who would later become known as one of the founders of cognitive psychology, had an opposing thesis: "These machines, when they work, are a theory of teaching." Galanter grasped that the ultimate value of teaching machines would be that they would reveal more about learning than humans had ever been able to observe before. "The study of teaching machine effectiveness is not, to us, an exercise in applied psychology," he wrote. "Rather, it is an experimental technique for the exploration of fundamental problems in the psychology of higher mental processes."[19]

One of the first to publish a vision for what computer-assisted instruction could be, Galanter did not want to simply create more aids for teaching. He wanted the machine to be able to surface what optimal teaching is. He wrote, "In current teaching technology, the plan of the machine, usually called the program, has been placed in the hands of a human designer. Our aim shall be to reduce this component of the machine's plan to a minimum. The result we anticipate is that when we understand how a machine's plans are formed, the problems that have been posed will evaporate. . . . [H]opefully, our results will serve as a plan to guide us in our experimentation so that the problems will in fact dissolve with a minimum of empirical flailing."[20]

Dismayed by what he saw as a lack of vision in the field of automated instruction, Galanter lamented that "many of the papers in this conference are concerned with these particular problems:

1. The programming problem—what is the correct order of presentation of material?
2. The error rate problem—is there an optimum number of errors that should be made?
3. The step size problem—how far apart should adjacent items of the program be spaced?"[21]

But one paper was radically different in how its authors proposed to address the challenges of creating optimal teaching. Researchers at IBM chose to write a program that simulated teaching and used a computer to power the software. In other words, IBM's teaching machine was simply software, a radical idea at the time. The authors wrote, "Our choice of a general-purpose digital computer for simulation of a teaching machine was guided by our desire for flexibility. This flexibility allows us to make changes in the teaching method without requiring that a new machine be built each time."[22] The shift from hardware—teaching machines, which were expensive to build and to buy—to software—programs that taught, which were easily and cheaply produced and sold—introduced the idea of education that was scalable to an extent that Pressey and Skinner could not have imagined.

IBM's presentation represented three major shifts in how automatic teaching would be viewed moving forward and created the model for how we define and think about educational technology today. The first major shift was the one from hardware to software: from teaching machines as different kinds of educational tools such as typewriters and calculators to teaching machines as software programs that can be run on existing machines—the computer. The second major shift assigned value to a computer's time and valued it higher than student time. (This was not surprising as one of IBM's business models was charging universities for time spent using the computer.) "Since the computer spends most of its time waiting for the student, suggestions for the utilization of this time are as follows: by multiplexing, the computer could present and score problems for several students who sat at different inquiry stations." The third major shift that built upon Skinner's vision of individualized instruction was the ability of the computer to "make decisions" and deliver adaptive learning: "the computer could be programmed to modify this order of presentation of problems by computing the difficulty of each problem as a function of students' performance."[23]

It wasn't long afterward that William Carr, a professor of psychology at Bucknell University, submitted a "a selective review of the recent literature dealing with self-instruction and the automation of teaching" to the Aerospace Medical Laboratory of the United States Air Force in August 1959. In his review, Carr identified "three major classes of variables which influence the effectiveness of learning by means of self-instructional devices": the device, the program, and the learner. Carr concluded that despite the exciting possibilities afforded by the computer software to provide superior teaching and learning, the human element was not so easily eliminated by the computer: "In any event, the sources of error which enter into the composing of a program used in a teaching device are precisely the same ones which enter into the use of standard pedagogic methods." Still, after his review of thirty-seven papers, Carr wrote, "It appears that when self-instructional devices are experimentally pitted against standard methods of instruction, the former prove to be the more effective."[24] Carr's findings neatly supported President Eisenhower's proposed investment in using computers to teach, which was pushed through Congress in reaction to a metal ball hurtling over the midwestern United States in 1957.

Balls in the Air

On October 4, 1957, the Russian satellite *Sputnik* sailed silently over the United States, emitting small pings as it went. About the size of a beach ball, the first satellite in orbit set off the space race. What was initially a curiosity for technophiles and space enthusiasts soon became a crisis as the public demanded President Eisenhower address the USSR's leap forward in technology and know-how.

But while Congress, the Senate and other government leaders scrambled to address this new development, a new, deeper fear took hold. What if the USSR's communist systems—particularly education—were superior to those of the United States? What if the Soviets were producing better-educated, smarter citizens? If that were true, the United States would soon be losing far more than the race to the moon; it would lose its supremacy in the world order.

These new concerns reignited old fears about the quality of U.S. education, particularly in math and science. How could the United States ensure that its educational systems were the best in the world? How could it guarantee that its students were the brightest? In the new space age, technology was king—and educational technology would soon become the newborn prince.

Up to this point, there had been significant resistance to federal aid for education, which was seen as socialist. But Senate Democrats knew they couldn't let a good crisis go to waste and so changed the name of the Education Act, which promised grants to students to pay for college, to the National Defense Education Act (NDEA)—making it a defense act and promising federally funded loans to students instead of grants.[25] This one act sowed the seeds that would eventually grow into today's student loan system and widespread use of educational technology. In 2012, fifty-five years later, iterations of these same educational technologies (in particular, MOOCs) were hailed as the solution to a problem the NDEA, and its successor, the Higher Education Act (HEA), also created—that of the "cost disease" of higher education and massive student loan debt.

Government Funding in Edtech

The U.S. government was instrumental in developing and expanding the uses of computers in education through significant investment in the form of research grants from a variety of sources, including the Office of Education (later the Department of Education), the National Science Foundation (NSF), and the Advanced Research Projects Agency (now DARPA), which funded experiments with military applications. This funding was part of a larger effort to create more students and research in areas that were critical to U.S. strategic interests during the Cold War.[26] The use of computers in education achieved at least two objectives that were useful to national security: rapidly scaling instruction in foreign languages and mathematics and advancing research in artificial intelligence.

The NDEA made money available to scientists and researchers at the same moment that there was a growing interest in using the computer to teach. For the first time, computers were available for research and experimentation in applications outside the military or business cases. Marvin Minsky, professor of computer science and codirector (along with Seymour Papert) of the Artificial Intelligence Lab at MIT, said, "Scientists only got computers in the late 1950s. There were the SEACs and the ENIACs (early computers) and things. It's only in 1957 when Fortran comes out that there are actually hundreds of people who get to use them."[27] The decade 1958–68 saw three major conditions that would enable the advancement of educational technology and computer-assisted instruction: the technology was available for use by researchers, the government was eager to spend money to develop these ideas, and public interest was sparked by the idea of "automatic teaching" that would provide individualized instruction.

In the decade after the passage of the NDEA, the Office of Education made $67 million in grants to universities across the country to experiment with using computers in education.[28] Although "automatic teaching" and later "computer-assisted instruction" (CAI) caught the country's attention, the bulk of grants made by the Office of Education were for managing and storing student data. In fact, overall, interest was low. According to Thomas Gallie, a program officer at NSF in 1968–69, "The problem was not money; it was people who were interested in doing research in the computer area." Gallie left NSF and established the computer science department at Duke. But as the years progressed, the problem persisted. "Many years later, when I was chairman of the computer science department at Duke, I tried to hire faculty members who worked in CAI. I couldn't find anybody in the country that wasn't already nailed down in Bitzer's shop or some place like that that seemed to me to be doing good academic research. And I finally just gave up."[29]

Andrew Molnar, a program officer for the Office of Education and for the NSF who was responsible for funding many of the experiments in computer-assisted instruction, concurs. "The early stages of computing were rather chaotic," he said. "Most were trying to demonstrate some application that could be used immediately.... While audio and graphics would be nice, most felt that they were just beyond the reach of education, and they did not want to wait for them to be widely available."[30] Institutions soon discovered that experiments were easy to start but difficult to scale. By the late 1960s government funding was drying up, in part because "we couldn't find enough good candidates for the money."[31] Several factors inhibited the growth of these programs, including lack of interest among professors and skilled staff to run the projects; however, one primary culprit was the structure of most universities, which were rarely conducive to product development, with a few notable exceptions.

Two universities did have significant CAI experiments: the University of Illinois and Stanford. Both were sustained by government grants but had very different relationships with funding. At Illinois, Don Bitzer, who was initially employed at Control Systems Laboratory—a classified military research lab at the university—was promoted to head a project that would enable a network of computers to serve up lessons and assessments to students. The project, PLATO (Programmed Logic for Automatic Teaching Operations), was heavily financed by ARPA (Advanced Research Projects Agency), which continued to build on the idea to create ARPANET (Advanced Research Project Agency Network), a series of connected terminals nationwide, which eventually became the internet. Stanford's approach was much more entrepreneurial by design. As Edward Feigenbaum, Stanford's first computer science department chair, noted, "Stanford was investing a lot of love and giving people openings and opportunities to make it on their own if they could, but was investing very few dollars. It seems to be a Stanford philosophy not to invest dollars, to invest a lot of love."[32] Pat Suppes found money from grants from the NSF, the Office of Education, and the Carnegie Corporation, and with Stanford's blessing he created the Institute for Mathematical Studies in the Social Sciences, which would create numerous experiments in CAI and significantly expand the field.[33]

Like Illinois, MIT also received funding from ARPA, and also had access to powerful computer hardware from IBM. But instead of using these resources to pursue CAI, Seymour Papert followed a different line of inquiry. Working with Marvin Minsky on artificial intelligence, Papert established a laboratory to observe children learning in order to inform how they might design computer, or machine, learning. Through these efforts with children, and building upon his years of work with Swiss psychologist Jean Piaget, a pioneer in the field of child development, Papert came to believe that the true power of the computer in education was in the student "teaching" or programming the computer, rather than the computer teaching (or programming) the student. On the whole, the group of scientists who were actively working to expand the capabilities of the computer, whether for education or military applications, was so small that, as Minsky put it, "one great feature was that if you discovered something you'd call them up the same day and say, hey I found this way to . . . we'd always be on the phone and I think there were no secrets."[34] Informal collaboration among the group continued for decades by trading the phone for a new technology from ARPANET: email.

The QWERTY Theory of Educational Technology

While working on the possibilities of integrating the computer into teaching and learning, Seymour Papert also identified a problem that would continue to impede the progress of educational technologies (computer-assisted instruction) for the next half century—what he called the QWERTY phenomenon. QWERTY are the six keys on the top left of a standard keyboard and were the top row of keys on a standard typewriter. As Papert explains, "The QWERTY arrangement has no rational explanation, only a historical one." In the early days of typewriter development, keyboards were laid out more rationally, with commonly used letters close together and the lesser used ones further apart. But the technology could not keep up with human use and the keys would jam. So the keyboard was redesigned to minimize the keys hitting each other by spacing out the most frequently used letters across the keyboard. A few years later, typewriter technology improved to the point where jamming was no longer a problem. Now what was stuck was the tradition of QWERTY. Papert described the reasons for maintaining QWERTY as follows: "Although these justifications have no rational foundation, they illustrate a process, a social process, of myth construction that allows us to build a justification for primitivity into any system.... We are in the process of digging ourselves into an anachronism by preserving practices that have no rational basis beyond their historical roots in an earlier period of technological and theoretical development."[35]

What Papert also described with QWERTY was the idea of human behavior shaping itself around technology. Papert wanted to flip the script so that technology served human behavior. He saw that we "justify primitivity in any system," including the educational system. For example, why do we put a chalkboard or whiteboard at the front of a classroom? Why do we reward the ability to sit still and passively listen for hours at a time? Why is college so expensive in terms of time and money? Many of our ideas of education are primitive compared to the context in which they are supposed to be relevant: our daily lives. With QWERTY, Papert identified two powerful forces, inertia and tradition, that have prevented evolution in education.

In fact, Bitzer, Papert, and Suppes pioneered not just ideas and methods for how the computer could be used in education but also, and potentially more importantly, what we could learn from the computer: not the computer as teacher but the computer as mindset—as a forcing function for systemic, rational thought. Today, this process of "thinking like a computer"—breaking down a problem or process into tiny, small discrete steps—is a good approach for problem-solving and has resulted in the automation of many processes. But it has also raised ethical considerations that we will be grappling with for some time: How does machine learning reflect our imperfections? When is artificial intelligence preferable to human intelligence and vice versa? How do we harness the enormous potential of AI to improve our lives? And what is its role in education?

2

Experimenting for the Future

All of these pioneers—Kemeny, Kurtz, Suppes, Atkinson, Bitzer and Papert—are significant not only because their conjectures about the use of computers openly question many of the assumptions upon which traditional education is based, but because they and their associates have explored a wide variety of computer-based environments that open new vistas and new ways of thinking about modern education.

—ANDREW MOLNAR

From Teaching Machines to Machine Learning

During the height of MOOC mania, when I was working at Coursera, university partners would often ask me, "What do all these computer scientists know about learning?" An answer was written by Seymour Papert in 1980, thirty-five years before the question was asked. He observed that AI can be defined narrowly as "extending the capacity of machines to perform functions that would be considered intelligent if performed by people" such as complex computation. But for Papert, more broadly, AI means defining and understanding the nature of the function you want the computer to do: "In order to make a machine capable of learning, we have to probe deeply into the nature of learning."[1]

Unusual for a mathematician, Papert had a strong background in human cognitive development. While working on his second doctorate at Cambridge, Papert ended up taking a job as a researcher for Jean Piaget at the International Centre of Genetic Epistemology at the University of Geneva, where he would spend five years, from 1959 to 1964. About the same time as Papert began working with Piaget, he met Marvin Minsky, a mathematics professor from MIT, when they gave almost exactly the same paper at a conference in London.[2] The two struck up a friendship, and Minsky began a multiyear recruitment effort to get Papert to come to MIT. Minsky did not see Papert's pivot from mathematics to child development and learning as a distraction; rather, Minsky felt it was critical to the project he and others at MIT were working on: artificial intelligence.

Papert came to MIT in 1964 as an associate professor of mathematics. Minsky quickly established the Artificial Intelligence Laboratory (AIL) and appointed himself and Papert as codirectors. The two received multiple grants from ARPA and NDEA to continue their work. Minsky said, "Just at the time that we were starting to need a lot of money for our own machines, '62–'63, then the Project MAC miracle happened and Project MAC got 3 million dollars a year and we got 1 million dollars a year. I don't recall ever writing a proposal for that."[3] They spent the money on a PDP-1 (the most powerful computer at the time, used at Stanford as well) and began their investigation into how computers could be programmed to replicate human learning. For the next fifteen years, they would document their efforts in a series of memos that they used to keep their colleagues and their funders apprised of their progress. As part of their work, Papert and Minsky persuaded MIT to create a children's learning environment in the same building that housed AIL and another highly influential initiative, the Laboratory for Computer Science (Project MAC). The idea was to promote the cross-pollination between the world of children and people thinking about children and education and the much smaller world of computers and computer scientists. The goal was not just to encourage new visions for education but also to help computer scientists understand the learning process. (They call it machine learning for a reason.) In fact, Marvin Minsky's highly influential book *The Society of Mind* (1988) came about from a strategy of thinking simultaneously about how children *do* think and how computers *might* think.

Papert was ultimately more influential than successful, at least by measures of income and career progress. But his influence on how to think about education and technology was truly profound. In 1971, Papert and Cynthia Solomon wrote "20 Things to Do with a Computer," which provided a radically different way of looking at technology used in education. In the piece, Papert operates from a set of principles and frameworks that were later seen as "the birth of the maker movement"[4] that continues today. He asks, "Why should computers in schools be confined to computing the squares of the first twenty odd numbers and similar so-called 'problem-solving uses?' Why not use them to produce some action?" Among the twenty uses are "Play Spacewar (#5)," "Have a Heart and Learn to Debug (#8)," "Write Concrete Poetry (#15)," and "Explain Yourself (#18)," each a far cry from the "drill and practice" origins of the original teaching machines.[5] Papert never gave up on his belief that the value of the computer was that it would serve as a mirror into our own mental processes. A decade after "20 Things" he would write, "The vision I have presented is of a particular computer culture . . . one that helps us not only to learn but to learn about learning."[6]

Seymour Papert Asks, "Who's the Boss?"

Papert's brilliant idea, which has highly relevant applications to today's AI-powered educational technologies, was that technology wasn't a replacement for teaching but was instead a tool for learning. He wrote, "In many schools today, the phrase 'computer-aided instruction' means making the computer teach the child. One might say the *computer is being used to program* the child. In my vision, *the child programs the computer*, and, in doing so, both acquires a sense of mastery over a piece of the most modern and powerful technology and establishes an intimate contact with some of the deepest ideas from science, from mathematics, and from the art of intellectual model building."[7]

Born in South Africa, Papert studied mathematics in Johannesburg and was equally fascinated by learning. He described himself as being utterly engrossed by cars when he was a toddler and felt that this captivation with auto mechanics gave him a mental model by which he could "assimilate" mathematical functions. (In other words, he was able to map mathematical principles to the workings of an automobile.) Papert felt strongly that his aptitude with mathematics was due, in part, to his having a concrete mental model (of a differential transmission) that he could attach to abstract concepts like algebra so he could more easily and quickly understand it. And like Skinner, Papert believed that the traditional classroom was not conducive to learning.

During work on his second doctorate, Papert met Jean Piaget when Piaget needed mathematical help on a project.[8] Piaget was the first to bring together child psychology and stages of learning, resulting in a reevaluation of traditional ideas of learning and education. Specifically, if a child's thought processes evolved over time, and on a fairly predetermined timetable, then reinforcement learning—or consistent repetition of concepts—was no longer viable if the child wasn't at the developmental stage that would enable him/her to grasp those concepts. Therefore, the role of the teacher was no longer simply to transmit knowledge but to guide the student to develop their own understanding of the concepts. Piaget called his theory of education "constructivism" and was hugely influential on Papert, who wrote, "I take from Jean Piaget a model of children as builders of their own intellectual structures."[9] In fact, Papert would develop his own educational theory, which he called "constructionism," that built upon Piaget's idea of children creating knowledge according to their mental models of the world. Swiss psychologist Edith Ackermann explains the relationship between constructivism and constructionism as follows: "Piaget's constructivism offers a window into what children are interested in, and able to achieve, at different stages of their development . . . Papert's constructionism, in contrast, focuses more on the art of learning, or 'learning to learn', and on the significance of making things in learning."[10]

Papert saw the mid-twentieth-century classroom "as an artificial and inefficient learning environment that society has been forced to invent because its informal environments fail in certain essential learning domains, such as writing or grammar or school math."[11] Like Pressey and Skinner before him, Papert saw the computer as a way to liberate the classroom from "inefficiencies." But unlike Pressey and Skinner, Papert felt that "automatic teaching" was a waste of the potential of the computer as an educational tool—and of the student's time. In his highly influential work, *Mindstorms* (1980), in which he describes over a decade of experimentation with computers in education, he writes, "Most of what has been done up to now under the name of 'educational technology' or 'computers in education' is still at the stage of the linear mix of old instructional methods with new technologies.... We are at a point in the history of education when radical change is possible, and the possibility for that change is directly tied to the impact of the computer."[12] Frustrated by what he saw as the waste of the computer to replicate existing, outmoded pedagogical approaches, Papert developed his own computer language, Logo, which enabled children to program simple robots, called "Turtles," as a way to learn by doing. Logo would become relatively popular over the next three decades as an educational software program, but its most transformational impact was reimagining John Dewey's approach of "learning by doing" with technology—and to broad acceptance for elementary education. Papert liberated learning from the classroom—at least the classrooms dependent upon paper, pencil, textbooks, chalk and chalkboard with the teacher at the front. By showing that children could be more engaged and self-aware through using technology as a tool, he laid the foundations not only for the maker movement in schools but also for the emerging field of artificial intelligence.

Suppes Dreams of a Tutor for Every Child

Pat Suppes couldn't wait for the computer to become "smart enough" to fulfill its potential as an infinitely patient and knowledgeable tutor, available to every child anywhere around the world. Growing up in Oklahoma, Suppes had two educational experiences that would inform his perspectives on, and experiments in, education over his lifetime. First, Suppes, who skipped a grade in elementary school, was part of a study that grouped gifted and talented students together and taught them an advanced curriculum in a competitive atmosphere. He would later describe this experience as "probably the single most important event of my intellectual life." Suppes relished the intensity of the program and the friends he made there, saying, "We enjoyed arguing and competing with each other and correcting the teacher when he was wrong."[13] His enjoyment of the program would inform many of his ideas about providing access to higher-level education to students without moving them forward a grade.

Second, and unique among those who pioneered computer-assisted instruction, Suppes was an early student of distance learning. After a peripatetic college career that had him enrolled at three different institutions over a few years, Suppes enlisted in the Air Force and reentered the University of Chicago as an Air Force cadet. Upon graduation, he was promptly sent to the Solomon Islands in Papua New Guinea, where, unarmed, and in his words "with a lot of free time," he began correspondence courses in advanced mathematics and French from the University of Chicago. In between writing meteorological reports and swimming, Suppes studied. The experience would shape his ideas about the potential for education at a distance for years to come.

After the war, Suppes worked in the oil fields as a wildcatter in Mexico, reading Aristotle in his truck at night.[14] He applied and was accepted to Columbia University where he graduated with a PhD in philosophy in 1950, and immediately began work at Stanford as an instructor in logic. Suppes's academic interests would span multiple departments over the course of his sixty-four years at Stanford, and he became a professor of philosophy with appointments in statistics, psychology, and education.

Like Skinner, Suppes became particularly interested in exploring education when his daughter was enrolled in elementary school. Dismayed by the instruction she was receiving in arithmetic, Suppes saw both the gaps in the instruction that was provided and the impossibility of asking the elementary school teacher to provide instruction tailored to meet every child's level. Rather than try to create an "automatic teacher," he spent his time developing an "automatic tutor" that would augment, not replace, classroom instruction, writing: "It should be emphasized, however, that no tutorial program designed in the near future will be able to handle every kind of problem that arises in student learning. It will remain the teacher's responsibility to attempt the challenging task of helping students who are not proceeding successfully with the tutorial program and who need special attention."[15]

But Suppes did not initially seek funding for computer-assisted instruction. Rather, he and Richard Atkinson (later the chair of NSF and president of the University of California System) were given a million dollars by the Carnegie Corporation. Suppes said, "Actually, we were invited to apply to build this automated laboratory for psychological investigations, experimental investigations with application to school learning, and other topics. That's how we got into computers—because we computed and then we realized we could do instruction with them."[16]

The laboratory, the Institute for Mathematical Studies in the Social Sciences (IMSSS), was directed by Suppes, Atkinson, and William K. Estes, one of B. F. Skinner's graduate students, with John McCarthy, "who founded the field of Artificial Intelligence,"[17] playing a role in the design of the laboratory. In fact, the first computer facilities were shared with McCarthy and his group, the Stanford Artificial Intelligence Laboratory (SAIL). The IMSSS grew quickly and gained the support of Fred Terman, Stanford's provost. Funding from the NSF and the Office of Education followed and, according to Suppes, "by '65, '66, I had almost two hundred people on campus working on these projects. I rounded up money here and rounded it up there. And we had a big activity, in many ways, the biggest in the country, on developing programs to use computers for instruction."[18]

In 1966, Suppes published "The Uses of Computers in Education," a notable article in *Scientific American* introducing his lab and its work in bringing mathematics education via computer to elementary schoolchildren in East Palo Alto. The piece described Suppes's experiments thus far, as well as his belief that "one can predict that in a few more years millions of schoolchildren will have access to what Philip of Macedon's son Alexander enjoyed as a royal prerogative: the personal services of a tutor as well-informed and responsive as Aristotle." Acknowledging this prediction as "extravagant," Suppes then acknowledged the "economic inefficiency" of the tutoring method, despite the widely held understanding that "the more an educational curriculum can adapt in a unique fashion to individual learners—each of whom has his own characteristic initial ability, rate and even 'style' of learning—the better the chance is of providing the student with a successful learning experience."[19]

The initial CAI experiments took place in 1965 in Palo Alto, where elementary school students answered arithmetic questions on a teletype machine that responded with instant feedback and a calculation of the students' score. The school sites and the students were chosen based on proximity to the campus and the willingness of the teachers to participate in the experiment. Proximity was important because the instructional machines were connected by telephone lines to a central computer on the Stanford campus so that student performance could be recorded and their data analyzed. These lessons were also adaptive; based on the students' performance the previous day, the program tailored instruction to the students' individual level to increase understanding. Some students were given these lessons as pre-work to prepare them for their teacher's instruction; other teachers used them as drill and practice for lessons already taught. In each case, the teacher determined how to best use the technology to blend the classroom so that it served student learning objectives.

Both students and teachers enjoyed working with the technology, and while the program was successful, expanding to schools in Mississippi, Kentucky, and Iowa in addition to the California schools over the next two to three years, it was ultimately too expensive and impractical to scale. The high cost and limited availability of the hardware meant the reach of computer-assisted instruction exceeded the grasp of easily available technologies by too wide a margin.[20]

Suppes realized that IMSSS activities not only had practical application in the classroom but also presented a business opportunity. Supported by Stanford's entrepreneurial culture and close ties with business, he founded a start-up: "In 1967, when computer-assisted instruction was still a very new educational technology, I organized with Richard Atkinson and others a small company, Computer Curriculum Corporation, to produce courses in the basic skills that are the main focus of elementary-school teaching."[21]

PLATO Connects Learners

In 1957, a young electrical engineer and PhD student named Don Bitzer was working at the Coordinated Science Laboratory, a classified military research lab at the University of Illinois. The son of a car salesman, Bitzer was a charming, energetic, and intelligent young man with an appetite for solving "impossible" problems. The lab's director, Daniel Alpert, a physics professor, was interested in teaching machines. (Alpert was influenced by Skinner's "heir conditioner" and even built one of his own which he used for his two daughters.) Alpert declassified all future lab projects so he could pursue projects exploring the educational potential of computers. A committee made up of professors of engineering and education was assembled to decide exactly what kind of project using computers for education the university should take on.

The committee was not successful. After a number of meetings in which productive conversation, creative ideation, and pragmatic problem-solving did not occur, Alpert threw up his hands and asked Bitzer, who had just finished his PhD, to spearhead the project. The education professors and their objections were ignored, and the engineers, led by Bitzer, tried to solve the problem of making the computer work for education.

Bitzer and Alpert envisioned a classic teaching machine, but one that was powered by one of the nation's most powerful computers: the ILLIAC 2, built at the University of Illinois and the first computer to use transistors instead of vacuum tubes. Funded by the military, with a grant from the Signal Corps, Bitzer used an old Magnavox TV he had lying around the house, hooked it up to a keypad, and used a phone line to connect it to ILLIAC 2. Students used the keyboard to connect to a bank

FIGURE 2. PLATO terminal with mathematical problem, ca. 1960. Courtesy of the University of Illinois Archives: RS 39/2/20, COL-13-13.

of slides on a given topic where they would be asked to fill in the blanks and would be assessed on their answers. The invention worked as a sort of shared workbook, where multiple students could connect to the same slide bank from their terminals and advance at their own speed. PLATO I may have been an odd-looking prototype, cobbled together with found objects, but it cracked open a world of possibilities about what a computer system could do to help instruction, providing the design basis for instruction at scale, particularly Massive Open Online Courses, fifty years later.

Bitzer was able to show that PLATO could be responsive to a student's own progress, but what was truly remarkable was that it could run with two simultaneous users. Two users may not seem like a huge increase, but it proved that PLATO II was scalable—that there could be multiple users sharing computer time and resources at a significant cost savings to the university. The possibility of truly scaling instruction had just been shown to be within reach.

Two years later, Bitzer debuted PLATO III, running on a more powerful CDC 1604 computer and enabling twenty users to work on the system simultaneously. PLATO III allowed for more enhanced instruction for the student, moving beyond the automatic workbook method of PLATO II to what Bitzer described as "inquiry teaching logics." He described the difference as follows: "An inquiry teaching logic permits a student to request information. The computer correctly interprets the request and replies from stored information or calculated results. This logic provides, in effect, a syntax for the student to use in communicating with the computer. The student is taught by composing his own requests." In practice, the computer served as "logic guardrails" for the student. For instance, if a student was creating a mathematical proof, the computer could evaluate whether each line of the proof was in line with mathematical principles—not if it was the correct answer. In fact, no correct answers were programmed, only the mathematical principles.[22]

This new method of instruction, which took advantage of improved computing power, offered tantalizing possibilities for instruction at scale. Bitzer spoke directly to the possibilities of providing education to previously unimaginable numbers of students in his 1965 report to his funders, ARPA and the Joint Services Electronic Programs (a collaboration among the Army,

Navy, and Air Force), writing: "There was no significant difference between the post-test scores of students who received instruction via PLATO system and those who attended regular class. However, the amount of time spent on the lesson material was significantly less for the students working on PLATO.... It was determined that a general-purpose computer, having a high-speed capacity of one million, five hundred thousand bits, would allow 1,000 students to be tutored concurrently on 8 different lessons without incurring a noticeable delay for any student's request."[23]

PLATO III was not just a successful proof of concept. It also defined the possibilities for computer-assisted education. The next iteration, PLATO IV, would introduce capabilities we take for granted today, including social networks, email, touch screens, and audio.

Bitzer had little problem funding the development of PLATO IV. He and his team gave live demonstrations to government agencies in Washington and obtained funding from the NSF and ARPA. His greatest challenges were engineering related: none of the hardware he needed to realize PLATO IV existed; he and his team had to build it themselves. First, though, they needed a computer powerful enough to support at least three hundred terminals, which was the basis for the NSF grant. Bitzer and Alpert took their problem to Bill Norris, CEO of CDC: "We said, Bill, what we have is a problem of wanting to pay zero up front, and the full rental rate at the end. Although this represents a large contribution by CDC, we think this participation in Computer Based Education will cost CDC less than attempting to go it alone and trying to develop their own system." Their pitch was successful, and they were able to get a 6400 computer on a five-year lease at a reduced rate. This was a win for both PLATO and CDC, but it was not an intentional snub to IBM. Says Bitzer, "If it had turned out that CDC didn't have what we needed and IBM did, we would have had to go with IBM." The agreement was not without cost, however. CDC obtained the license to make and sell hardware and software innovations developed by the PLATO program.[24]

One of the first, and perhaps the best known, invention that was a by-product of PLATO IV was the plasma display, which became standard in flat-screen televisions for the next forty years. The instruction manual for PLATO IV describes it as follows: "The physics of the plasma panel is such that the panel itself has a memory." This capability was significant because it meant that the display did not need to use computer memory after the image was first displayed. The computer only needed to use memory when the display changed. This savings in computer time, although small, permitted additional users to share the main terminal: "The computer is free to converse with other terminals and do other jobs until a change in the display is required."[25] Bitzer and H. G. Slottow filed a patent for this invention in 1964, and it is the one that Bitzer is most famous for as an engineer.

As work continued productively in Bitzer's lab, the university wrestled with questions of governance and control. In 1966, the university established CERL (Computer-based Education Research Laboratory) as "a unit of the Graduate College ... and was organized into a Technical Systems Development Group to cooperate with PLATO, an Operating Group, and an Educational Development Group."[26] This took PLATO out of military research (classified or declassified) and moved it into the more central academic structure. Bitzer was busy traveling and promoting PLATO. And while he promoted the educational possibilities of what he was now calling "computer-enabled instruction," he was also clear-eyed about the cost, unlike many of his peers in CAI. Thomas Gallie, program officer in the Office of Computing Activities of the NSF, said, "Bitzer was the only person in the country that I know of at the time (1969) who had the courage and intelligence to talk in a forthright way about what it would cost to deliver CAI, and what the cost had to be to compete with human labor."[27]

In 1970, Bitzer and Alpert published an article in the journal *Science*, "Advances in Computer-Based Education." In it, they introduced PLATO to a broader audience and described their two main objectives for their work:

1) Investigation of the potential role of the computer in the instructional process. The major objective of this phase has been to examine the question, What is educationally possible?
2) Design of an economical and educationally viable system incorporating the most valuable approaches to teaching and learning.[28]

It seemed as though Bitzer and Alpert had methodically, and with flashes of brilliance, solved the problem of automated instruction at scale. The release of PLATO IV in 1972 supported this impression. PLATO IV was a technological marvel and a huge advance in human computer interaction. It featured a touch screen and a way to communicate with other users (a precursor to email) and could "speak" to the student through preprogrammed audio messages, which were useful for teaching languages or medical instruction, among other things. PLATO IV's instruction manual described it this way: "The terminal will show you pictures, drawings, and writing; it will give you messages to which you can listen. It also responds to touching: it's a sensitive thing, you know. The terminal is your means for interacting with the educational system called PLATO."[29]

The financial implications of PLATO IV were immediately understood by the university, which transferred administrative jurisdiction of CERL from the Graduate College to the Office of the Vice Chancellor for Academic Affairs on February 1, 1973, "because the PLATO system was considered well-developed and relevant to the entire campus."[30] It also stood to make the university and Control Data Corporation a great deal of money.

The Education-Industrial Complex

When the Mansfield Amendment and things started, and we had to start writing complicated proposals to ARPA justifying what we were doing and had to find some relevance, things like that. It got to be rather painful. . . . Eventually Papert and I quit, because we couldn't stand that, having to be able to manage it.

—MARVIN MINSKY, 1989

And then, just as political sentiment created the funding for computers in education, political sentiment took it away. Late in 1969, Senator Mike Mansfield (D-WA) introduced an amendment to the Military Authorization Act that barred the Defense Department from using its funds "to carry out any research project or study unless such project or study has a direct and apparent relationship to a specific military function."[31] This amendment was part of an overall strategy to curtail money flowing to the military and to separate academic research from military funding and had an immediate effect on DOD funding of educational technologies. The money spigot that had been turned on in the aftermath of *Sputnik* was now being closed off because of the unpopularity of the Vietnam War. Those projects that had been funded by DOD were supposed to have been taken up by the National Science Foundation. But the NSF's budget was not increased by the same amount that the DOD funding was.

Some scientists gave up. Suppes and Bitzer got creative. All three professors were awarded NSF funding by Andrew Molnar, and Suppes pursued "spinning out" his technology to a privately owned company, the Computer Curriculum Corporation, while Bitzer and the University of Illinois signed a contract with CDC that licensed the rights to sell PLATO's hardware and software inventions.[32] Ironically, Papert, who had access to arguably the most sophisticated and expensive computers in the country at the time, did not have much use for them. Bitzer and Suppes, however, were absolutely dependent upon computing power. Writes Suppes, "Without the sophisticated computer facilities available to me at Stanford it would not have been possible to pursue these matters in such detail and on such a scale."[33] Both the expense and limited availability of powerful computers would create business partnerships that took PLATO and Suppes's work in new directions that focused more on marketability than research.

Papert was a mathematician and educational theorist, Suppes was a philosopher and logician, and Bitzer was an engineer. They came from different social classes, countries, and states and brought a heterogeneous set of experiences to the central problem of each of their early careers: how to make the computer work to enhance instruction. There is not much evidence that the three socialized, although they certainly knew each other as colleagues and peers. Bitzer and Suppes presented together on a number of occasions and, by all accounts, respected each other and the work they were doing. Their respective research domains were not only complementary but also overlapped. Says Adele Goldberg, who worked with both systems, "You have a classroom with closets at the back of the room, and the idea was that there were two PLATO terminals, one in each closet, and the students would rotate to go back for their 15 or 20 minutes, which wasn't all that much different from what we were doing at Stanford."[34] Suppes's CAI terminals were connected by phone line to McCarthy's PDP-1, while Bitzer's terminals were connected to the mainframe 6400 in Illinois.

Papert, by all accounts a kind and "impish" man,[35] didn't appear to hold Suppes and Bitzer's work in much esteem. In "20 Things to Do with a Computer," #16 is "Try CAI and Psychology" and includes, "The conclusion from all this is that we have at last discovered the true role of CAI in education. Writing CAI programs is one of the twenty best projects for the first semester of a fifth-grade computer science course!"[36] Even the publication of "20 Things" can be seen as a response to "Uses of Computers in Education" in *Scientific American* from Suppes and Bitzer's "Advances in Computer-Based Education" in *Science*. But Papert and Suppes respected one another, and Papert acknowledged him as one of "a few people with whom disagreements about how computers should be used have always been valuable: John Seeley Brown, Ira Goldstein, Robert Davis, Arthur Leauhrman, Patrick Suppes."[37] Papert surely knew of PLATO and Bitzer, but he did not write or speak about it publicly.

While Papert saw computers as tools students manipulated in order to learn about learning, and Suppes pushed existing technologies to fulfill the vision of personalized education, Bitzer had a vision for an entire networked computer—the internet, community, whose initial topic was education. PLATO was a computer system that happened to do education. With engineering brilliance, autonomy, and a great deal of government money, Bitzer was able to realize Skinner's vision of automatic teaching more so than Suppes or Papert. Yet, Suppes would ultimately have the longest career in CAI, publish the most extensively, and make the most money, while Papert's inspiration and influence may be most important in considering education's incorporation of artificial intelligence today.

3

Commercialization

> Many new technologies come with a promise to change the world, but the world refuses to cooperate.
>
> —HENRY PETROSKI

Government money for computer-assisted instruction and artificial intelligence dried up in the 1970s, and while AI research entered a dry season called "AI Winter," Patrick Suppes, Don Bitzer, and Seymour Papert looked outside their universities to business for funding to keep their inventions alive. In Palo Alto, Suppes tried in vain to find commercial backing for his adaptive tutoring software. Bob Smith, one of his PhD students-turned-employee, recalled, "The system was also extremely expensive, unwieldy, didn't work and required two operators in the back room. Now IBM decided that this wasn't going to work—it was too expensive, it was too early; they convinced Pat to commercialize it."[1] Suppes formed the Computer Curriculum Corporation with fellow professor Richard Atkinson and ran the company for the next two decades while maintaining a full teaching load.[2] In Champaign, Bitzer and the University of Illinois signed a contract that gave the Computer

Data Corporation the rights to distribute PLATO IV. In Cambridge, Papert continued to refine Logo and its Turtles, eventually partnering with Lego to mass-produce a version of self-assembled and programmed "robots" that were in production until 2021.[3] These attempts were moderately successful; however, their success paled in comparison to that of broader efforts to commercialize a much more expensive educational product: the college degree.

The notion that a college degree was an investment measured in lifetime earnings that justified an individual taking on debt was a subtle but significant shift that would transform the business of higher ed, enable the rise of for-profit universities, result in the student loan crisis, and create the conditions for another "automagic" technology solution thirty years later: MOOCs. In the 1980s, several factors helped change the public perception of universities as institutions that should be supported by federal dollars, including economic policies (particularly supply-side economics), which focused on reducing taxes and regulations to stimulate economic growth. (Previous decades emphasized government spending and intervention in the economy following Keynesian policies.) Concurrently, the 1980s saw a focus on standards and accountability, with policies aimed at improving the quality of education and holding schools accountable for student performance, resulting in the expansion of standardized testing and school choice initiatives.[4]

At the same time, tuition costs for higher education in the United States began to rise significantly. This trend was driven by a variety of factors, including reductions in state funding for public universities, increased operating costs for institutions, and a growing demand for higher education. Yet the ability of lower- and middle-class students to borrow money for college was capped by borrowing limits for federal loans, just as demand for higher education was expanding, particularly among demographics who had been discouraged from attending previously: minorities, adults, and women.[5] These conditions transferred more of the financial investment in education from the government to individuals, many of whom, quite rationally, saw that investment as one that should provide returns in the form of increased wages.[6]

Concurrently, research funds and interest in artificial intelligence were also in decline. In the 1970s, the reach of those trying to expand the capabilities of the computer exceeded the grasp of the hardware—what the computer could actually do. Combined with the availability of government money only for those projects that had a clear military application, the computer, with its relatively primitive capabilities, became less interesting to scholars just as it became more interesting to business. The field was also in flux theoretically. At MIT, Papert and Minsky were questioning whether the model of neural networks (or the human brain) was the right one to use as a basis for artificial intelligence. In their groundbreaking work, *Perceptrons*, Minsky and Papert illustrated the problems with using such a model and, in doing so, began to lower the temperature on the overheated claims of technology's abilities. "We know shamefully little about our computers and their computations," they wrote. "This seems paradoxical because physically and logically, computers are so transparent in their principles of operation."[7]

A period known as "AI Winter" soon followed, a season of skepticism about artificial intelligence that began with a report by James Lighthill, a professor at Cambridge University, titled "Artificial Intelligence: A General Survey."[8] Lighthill argued that AI research should be more tightly coupled to practical problem-solving rather than pursuing overly ambitious theoretical goals. His findings reflected the aims of the UK government body that commissioned the report, the Science Research Council (SRC), which wanted to ensure that research in AI was tightly coupled to practical problem-solving, aligning with broader national interests. But the absence of adequate computing power and infrastructure hindered the ability to achieve the ambitious goals set by AI researchers, and so failure to solve practical problems with this new technology was almost certainly guaranteed.[9] In fact, when computing power eventually did increase, so did interest in artificial intelligence and neural networks. In the foreword to the 2017 reissue of *Perceptrons*, Leo Botton writes, "When they wrote *Perceptrons*, Minsky and Papert clearly did not anticipate that the mere passage of time would eventually tilt the balance in favor of learning systems."[10] The basis for Lighthill's condemnation: that there was not enough connection between the practical applications of AI—advanced automation—and the scholarly pursuit of AI as a model for intelligence—cognitive simulation—is based on a similar model that scholarship should be measured according to its value to industry.

In the midst of these shifts in financing and perception, Stanford, MIT, and Illinois moved ahead with using learning technologies to connect to industry, expand influence, transmit democracy internationally, make money, disrupt traditional education models, "change the world," expand access, and create new forms of K–12 education. As the government was offering less funding, technology was showing promise in distributing knowledge and creating connections. These universities took advantage of these opportunities, in part, to reduce their reliance on public monies. The era of educational entrepreneurship was in full swing.

Using Technology to Connect to Industry: Stanford Instructional Television Network

Stanford's experiments in using the technology to enable distance learning were not limited to Suppes and Atkinson. In 1969, Joseph M. Pettit, a former student of Frederick Terman and his successor as dean of the School of Engineering, led a group of Stanford engineers in using television to deliver education as part of the Stanford Instructional Television Network (SITN). Generally, the use of television for transmitting education was part of Stanford's broader strategy to position itself as a leading institution in the field of engineering education and to secure federal support for its instructional programs. Specifically, SITN was designed to address the logistical challenges of transporting employed students to and from Stanford's Palo Alto campus during the workday. Television enabled Stanford to provide continuing education to engineers and other professionals in the local high-tech industry, and by 1974, two-thirds of SITN's revenue came from nondegree students, comprising 87 percent of course registrations over the network. This innovative approach also allowed Stanford to generate additional revenue by charging peer institutions for access to SITN facilities and off-peak airtime. SITN was eventually replaced by the Stanford Center for Professional Development (SCPD), which continues to provide distance learning opportunities today.[11]

Using Technology to Expand Influence: The Computer Curriculum Corporation

The Computer Curriculum Corporation (CCC) was formed at the suggestion of IBM, who encouraged Pat Suppes to commercialize the software programs his group was creating for

CAI at Stanford. Suppes and Dick Atkinson decided to move forward with the project and incorporated in the summer of 1967. At first, they produced courses in basic skills for elementary schoolchildren, building on the curriculum developed for the first CAI experiments in elementary schools in East Palo Alto. By his own admission, Suppes said, "we were lucky to survive the first five or six years."[12] But by the early to mid-1970s the company was on more solid footing, with a core staff who remained with the company for decades and had a reputation for "high standards, high ethics, and fun." Suppes was quite involved with CCC and would visit prospective customers and also bargain with computer hardware companies to make hardware that was less expensive for school systems to purchase.

One factor in CCC's success was that it was primarily a software corporation, which made it easier for the company to be market responsive (software is much cheaper and quicker to manufacture than computer hardware). CCC wrote software that ran on computers from IBM, HP, UNIVAC, SLS, and others. The programs increased in complexity as computing power became more accessible. CCC eventually built its own system, but the cost was prohibitive at approximately $10,000 per terminal. Still, the company was thriving. After two decades of success, Suppes began to think about the next phase of his career. Ron Fortune, CCC's president, recalled, "In '87, Pat said, 'I've been at this for twenty-plus years at CCC and another ten years' work at Stanford. I'm ready to monetize.... The market crashed, it didn't happen."[13] Despite the crash, CCC was an attractive target for acquisition. By 1990, CCC was in 4,000 schools, had issued 400,000 licenses, had 350 employees, and was bringing in $35 million in revenue a year. It was acquired by Simon and Schuster for a reported $60 million.

While leading CCC, Suppes also continued to head up the Institute for Mathematical Studies in the Social Sciences (IMSSS) at Stanford. From 1968 to 1980, IMSSS was involved in curriculum development, software development, and educational research and received a fair bit of the scarce NSF funding available during the decade.

The breadth of the research efforts at IMSSS was impressive. The institute began its program of research and development in computer-assisted instruction in 1963 with a program that consisted of two lessons in elementary mathematical logic for four students (who completed twenty-three total exercises). As this program scaled over the years, it presented a central problem that Suppes and his colleagues would spend decades working on: programming the computer so that it could check the mathematical proof submitted by a student. While the mathematical proof was relatively easy to program at the elementary school level, interactive theorem-proving at the university level was a much more difficult challenge (and one that was the subject of many papers on interactive theorem-proving in CAI courses). An introductory logic course developed at IMSS was taken by thousands of students during its time, which gave Suppes the honor of having the highest number of students at Stanford.[14]

Another main research focus of Suppes and the IMSSS during this time was "digital speech" or the ability for the computer to respond to questions posed by a student (much like Siri, Alexa, and Google do today). Suppes was still trying to create the "automatic tutor" and felt that the computer absolutely had to be able to converse with the student in order for this vision to be realized. The early CAI systems used prerecorded messages that were served to the student at the appropriate time, but the experience for the learner was suboptimal. Suppes outlined "three good reasons" for devoting IMSSS resources to the study of digital speech. First, it was difficult to get reliability from the tape devices; second, it was too difficult to get tape devices that provided sufficiently fast seek times to retrieve prerecorded messages; and third, "it was ultimately unsatisfactory to use, without exception, prestored messages." Researchers at the IMSSS soon turned their attention to developing speech-recognition systems "because of the great significance of such techniques for instructional purposes."[15] This research resulted in an experiment called "Dial a Drill," which used a relatively inexpensive and widely available technology, the telephone, to provide instruction at a distance. While the researchers in Suppes's group at Stanford were working on developing speech recognition over the telephone, Suppes's Computer Curriculum Corporation was marketing Dial a Drill to school systems in one of many examples of the synergy between research and development at IMSSS and the market developed by CCC. The early Dial a Drill programs were quite simple. The student would be asked "What is 7 minus 3?" over the telephone. If the child pressed the number "4" she would be given the next question. If she was wrong the computer would correct her.

Dial a Drill Example

Computer (via phone): *Welcome to Dial-A-Drill. Please type your number followed by the pound key.*
[Student types 1425#.]

Hi Jon Jones. Let's continue your math lesson. Listen to the exercise, then type the answer followed by the pound key. 7 +2=
[Student types 9#.]

Great! 3 + 8 is . . .
[Student types 10#.]

Sorry, that is wrong. Please try again.
3 + 8 is . . . [16]

This same technology was applied to foreign-language learning and programs in Russian, French, Armenian, and Arabic were used by Stanford students for decades. Suppes and the institute published a prodigious amount of research, which raised his experiments in CAI to a wider academic audience, even as some educational theorists, particularly Papert, criticized Suppes's CAI experiments as being rooted in behaviorism and "programming the child." However, Suppes saw great potential in CAI for raising the quality and availability of instruction for every child, regardless of socioeconomic circumstances. And in time, so did the U.S. Agency for International Development (USAID).

Using Technology to Transmit Democracy: The Nicaragua Radio Mathematics Project

In the early 1970s USAID contacted Suppes and his team and asked if principal design elements of CAI's interactive curriculum could be replicated using a cheaper and more widely available technology to help scale education globally. "We worked on computers, but then USAID asked if we could use radio, because it was cheaper," said Suppes.[17] After an initial survey of several potential sites, Nicaragua was chosen, and the Nicaragua Radio Mathematics Project (NRMP) began in earnest.

And so in 1975, ten years after fourth-grade students in Palo Alto–area schools had completed daily drill-and-practice arithmetic lessons in their classroom on a teletype machine connected by telephone lines to a computer on the Stanford campus, first-grade students in sixteen classrooms outside Managua, Nicaragua, were listening to a twenty-minute mathematics lesson on the radio while responding verbally, physically, and by writing answers on a worksheet to questions posed during the broadcast. Those worksheets were brought to a central location in Managua where they were entered into a computer by punch cards. Those cards were fed into the computer and their data stored on magnetic tape; those tapes were sent by international mail to Stanford where the data was analyzed on the computer there. This data was used to refine the lessons to be more effective. The data transfer from Nicaraguan schoolroom to Stanford campus took approximately one week; curriculum changes could be made during the course of the school year. It is interesting to note that in the years of operation no data was ever lost in the mail.

Growing political instability in Nicaragua in 1978 precipitated the withdrawal of U.S. government funding for the project, and Stanford funding followed suit. Yet while the project lay dormant in Nicaragua, the principles and methodologies of NRMP were adapted and expanded over the next forty years to include Interactive Radio Instruction (IRI) across a range of topics from mathematics, language, science, and reading among others (to date, over twenty million learners in primarily poorer and/or densely populated countries across the globe have used IRI in the classroom). This design model of scalable, active learning was rediscovered and replicated in the twenty-first century in a number of popular educational technologies, including Khan Academy and its offshoots, adaptive learning programs, and MOOCs themselves. Just as importantly, these projects helped pioneer the practice of collecting student data to measure effectiveness of instruction and allow for curricular changes during the instruction period as well as to individualize instruction based on performance.[18]

Of the three main players in CAI, Suppes alone was able to succeed in both the business and academic worlds, operating both a successful commercial venture and a thriving research and development group at Stanford. His success was due in part to the culture at Stanford, which gave him the freedom and encouragement to have a dual role as entrepreneur and scholar. Papert struggled with commercialization and building a bridge between his educational theory of constructionism and the rest of the education academic community.

However, Bitzer at Illinois was involved in research and saw its value in informing the refinements to PLATO IV and its best uses, but he did not pursue research himself as thoroughly as Suppes: "At heart, Bitzer was an engineer and a used car salesman," said historian Brian Dear.[19] He was an inventor and a salesperson, a brilliant engineer, charismatic, passionate, and energetic, who cared deeply about education and also about the many engineering inventions he and his students produced.

Using Technology to Make Money: PLATO IV

> PLATO widens your child's world. Announcing new educational courseware for microcomputers to improve your child's Basic Skills, High School Skills, or Foreign Language Vocabulary.
>
> —CDC ADVERTISEMENT FOR PLATO, 1982

The contract to manufacture and distribute PLATO IV was officially signed by Control Data Corporation (CDC) and the University of Illinois in 1976, but the company had been deeply

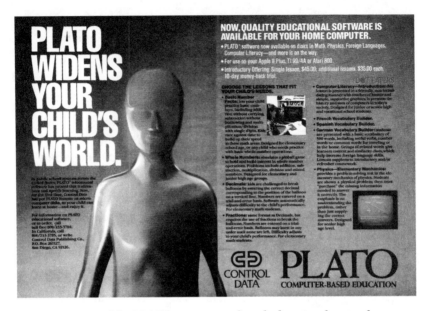

FIGURE 3. Ad for PLATO, a computer-based educational system by Control Data Corporation, 1982, from Citizens of PLATO Digital Archive, https://umsi580.lsait.lsa.umich.edu/s/PLATOs-Citizens/item/1848.

involved in the development of PLATO IV for the previous two to three years to ensure it was a commercially viable product. Don Bitzer recalled, "They had engineers looking at terminal designs. Others were integrating the computers into the system. How will the machines fit together? Some were involved in software development with us. That started almost as soon as PLATO IV was in operation using several hundred terminals."[20] PLATO IV seemed poised for commercial success. CDC invested heavily in a large sales staff and produced print and radio ads touting the capabilities of the new system.

PLATO IV's main customers were universities and school systems. Personal computers were still largely unavailable and expensive for the vast majority of households; selling directly to parents who were anxious about their children's education was still few years away. Unfortunately, PLATO IV was too expensive for most college campuses as well. And there were stipulations in the original contract that led to the deterioration of the relationship between Illinois and CDC. Still, CDC had a potential gold mine in PLATO IV because the product was so effective and revolutionary in its capabilities. Given the company's investment in sales and marketing, it seemed as though PLATO IV was poised to be in almost every school system and higher education institution in the country and the world. But CDC was undone, in part, by the cost of the system and by its own efforts to separate from Illinois.

CDC and Illinois had an agreement that the university could continue to sell PLATO terminals and service to institutions that met three criteria: (1) they were grandfathered in as previous customers, (2) they were using PLATO IV to conduct educational research, and (3) the institution had four or fewer terminals. Once an institution wanted to move beyond four terminals, then CDC would try to upsell them a full PLATO system. This system worked well enough, but inevitably, frictions arose. According to Bitzer, "It has been clumsy in some cases. Remote locations have the largest phone line costs, yet they share only four terminals in a line which could support sixteen terminals. The communication costs could be reduced considerably by connecting sixteen terminals. It was difficult for the school to understand why we would not allow them to expand."[21]

By the time CDC assumed full control of PLATO IV, Bitzer and his group had already created a substantial number of educational partners and users. The group at Illinois prepared a 1977 report to the NSF to describe their progress. NSF had provided some support for a "major expansion, implementation and evaluation" of the system, with one objective being creating a geographically dispersed network serving at least five hundred individual consoles across several institutions. The work of the PLATO group easily surpassed this objective, reporting, "From a beginning of ten terminals on PLATO IV in January 1972, the number has grown to about 950, with up to 500 active simultaneously. The sites are scattered across the Continental United States; one terminal is in Sweden, and terminals have been connected for demonstration in the Soviet Union, Italy, Rumania, Venezuela, Sweden, France, Germany, and Iran.... [O]ver 20,000 students are using the system. For the past two years system usage has exceeded one million terminal hours per year."[22] By 1976, PLATO IV was being used in elementary schools, with courses in mathematics and reading; in community colleges with courses in accounting, biology, chemistry, English, and mathematics; and at universities with courses in chemistry and physics. Because the PLATO Group at Illinois had created a new language, called TUTOR, to enable instructors to create their own courses, new curricular material was added frequently, with over 2,000 instructors and curriculum developers working to create content for the system. The PLATO Group at Illinois produced a help center that answered 600,000 questions in 1975.

PLATO IV was a truly remarkable effort. Besides creating new hardware, components of which (the plasma display panel and the touch screen, among others) would have been groundbreaking on their own, Bitzer and his team invented new software, new systems for delivering computer-based education, new implementations of those systems, new media (using computer graphics), new ways to conduct educational research, and a programming language (TUTOR) so that teachers and curriculum experts could create their own material to run on the system. And then the PLATO Group created a method for scaling support of their hardware and software, all while attracting nearly a thousand institutional customers.

But for all of the PLATO Group's successes, CDC was unable to use this strong foundation to build a profitable business. One problem was the company's decision to invest in rewriting curriculum that had already been created and tested by professors and developers. Says Bitzer, "But the courseware agreements had several problems. CDC decided to go into competition with the University of Illinois authors. They opened their own courseware development in similar areas, and they wanted exclusive rights to the courseware developed at the university." As a result, CDC ended up spending hundreds of thousands of dollars in developing curriculum that had already been developed, tested, and accepted by their customers. Another hurdle was CDC's struggle to convince schools to make the leap from piloting four terminals at a low cost to purchasing a full system at a much higher price. As Bitzer recalled, "We couldn't expand to very large numbers and CDC didn't know how to handle small users.... I would say that after you use four terminals successfully that you need sixteen to be productive and cost-effective. It just didn't make any sense.... At the four-terminal level for an educational institution, CDC couldn't afford to run the experiments to nourish the new institutions. Many CDC salesmen did not know what PLATO could do. Small sites needed special care to expand."[23]

Ultimately, CDC was not able to overcome its high curriculum costs and sales model. By the mid-1980s the company would invest nearly a billion dollars in PLATO[24] and was eager to generate higher returns. In pursuit of profitability, CDC began pursuing personal computer owners. Yet despite significant investment in advertising, PLATO IV failed to gain traction in the personal computing market. CEO William Norris retired in 1986, and the PLATO trademark and courseware were sold to the Roach Organization in 1989. The University of Illinois created a commercial unit called NovaNET to market and service PLATO to customers, which became the primary distributor of PLATO IV in the decades to come.[25]

Don Bitzer retired from the University of Illinois in 1989. His attempts to keep PLATO functioning in schools under the NovaNET name had created an administrative tangle that consumed a target portion of his time. Bitzer wanted to act as CEO of NovaNET and obtain funds from venture capitalists, but the University of Illinois was not as practiced as Stanford in creating the space necessary for professors to also be entrepreneurs and business owners in the private sector. Ultimately, the situation became untenable, and Bitzer accepted a position at North Carolina State University as a distinguished university research professor in computer science. He won an Emmy award in 2002 for the invention and development of plasma displays.

NovaNET foundered without Bitzer. While a core group of users remained devoted to the system, it was soon outpaced and overpowered by new software that ran on personal computers and by learning communities on the internet. Technology historian Brian Dear writes, "With ever-more-powerful microcomputers and the rise of online services . . . and of course, the growing internet, there were now copious alternatives to PLATO. There was also an increasing variety of ways to bring PLATO ideas and ways of thinking, the system's features, lessons, notefiles and games, to these alternative platforms."[26] National Computer Systems acquired NovaNET Learning in 1999 and was itself acquired by Pearson in 2000. NovaNET reached its fullest potential at Pearson with a peak of over 13,000 simultaneous users in 2008. But just two years later, NovaNET's performance was less impressive, and rumors began circulating that it was planned to be shut down.

Using Educational Technology as a Tool for Learning

In Papert's eyes, the computer was an object to think with. He built a bridge between progressive educational traditions and the Internet age to maintain the viability of schooling, and to ensure the democratization of powerful ideas.[27]

While Papert's innovation, scholarship and wisdom is widely recognized across the globe and among scientists, his half century of contributions to his major field of choice, education, is largely invisible. It is not that educators disagree with Papert's theories or recommendations, they just ignore him entirely.[28]

At MIT, Papert and Minsky continued their research into AI but began to focus more on robotics and less on perceptrons or neural networks. Meanwhile, Papert's interest in educational philosophy and his theory of constructionism grew with the further development of Logo. He was named the Cecil and Ida Green Professor of Education at MIT in 1974 and served in this role until 1981, shortly after his seminal work, *Mindstorms*, was published. Along with colleagues in the Logo group, Papert founded Logo Computer Systems, Inc. (LCSI), which maintains a web presence today. LCSI served as a commercialization channel for Logo, and Papert designed several notable programs for LCSI, including LogoWriter and what would become Lego Mindstorms.

Despite his accomplishments and influence on education technology, Papert faded from the discussion of computers in education. "Still, even as Papert's ideas continue to crop up in software and his writing continues to be read in classes at the MIT Media Lab and beyond he is indeed less commonly discussed in schools of education."[29] Papert's view that children were to teach computers, as opposed to computers teaching children, was groundbreaking and his home institution, MIT, was nearly unparalleled in prestige, yet the adoption and scale of his ideas never achieved significant momentum because they suffered from two fatal flaws. First, Papert subscribed to the model that most schools are teaching factories, stamping out identically taught students with no regard to individual learning differences.[30] And second, Papert held conflicting views about teachers. His general anti-authoritarianism, antitraditional school stance often led him to disparage teachers as cogs in the educational machine while at the same time encouraging them to think independently and experiment with Logo. Both these views, informed by the "hacker culture" prevalent at MIT, would impede Logo's success in educational realms. Papert would never realize the traditional academic or commercial success of Suppes or Bitzer.

While Bitzer and Suppes enjoyed the entrepreneurial business challenges of bringing their CAI inventions to market, Papert was more interested in the process of changing people's minds about education than in the process of commercialization. Because Logo was a programming language, Papert and LCSI were able to deal directly with computer manufacturers to include Logo as part of the software package that came with the computer, rather than selling their software directly to school systems, as Suppes and Atkinson's CCC did. "In 1978 Papert was contacted by Cecil Green of Texas Instruments. TI wanted a version of Logo for the upcoming TI 99/4," writes Cynthia Solomon, a co-developer of Logo. "The TI 99/4 was

COMMERCIALIZATION 75

Text from the poster:
"Is it possible to make a more direct attack on teaching children to think?

Seymour Paper will survey the state of knowledge and describe an unorthodox plan for elementary education.

Marvin Minsky will direct a discussion with Robert Davis, Allen Newell and Patrick Suppes. The goals are to disseminate information, to provoke discussion and to recruit collaboration."

FIGURE 4. Poster of the first public Logo symposium (April 11, 1970), called 'Teaching Children Thinking,' held at MIT. Over 700 people attended this gathering which featured Seymour Papert, Marvin Minsky, and Patrick Suppes. *Source:* Cynthia Solomon collection. Cynthia Solomon et al., "History of Logo," *Proceedings of the ACM on Programming Languages* 4, HOPL (2020): 1–66. https://web.media.mit.edu/~lieber/Publications/History-of-Logo.pdf.

the first microcomputer with Logo on it available to schools and homes."[31] Unfortunately, it was a commercial failure, although it provided key modifications that allowed the program to develop into object-oriented programming. But at the same time, LCSI developed a version of Logo for the Apple II computer called Apple Logo. Of the 303 versions of Logo cataloged in the Logo Tree Project almost all are descendants of either the TI Logo (and a sister version for Apple) designed by the MIT Logo Group or Apple Logo developed by LCSI. The University of California, Berkeley, created UCBlogo in 1988 as an open-source software, and many subsequent versions were built on this free code.[32]

In 1980, Papert's best-selling book, *Mindstorms*, was released, which brought Papert's theory of constructionism to a wider audience and remains the core reference on the subject. *Mindstorms* is credited with influencing robotics movements and maker spaces, as well as with popularizing the idea that the teacher's role was to activate a student's love of learning—what Papert described as a passion—and using that passion as a foundation for other types of learning such as in mathematics, languages, and so forth. A central theme of *Mindstorms* is the idea of "debugging"—that is, finding the errors in your work and correcting them—as the key to teaching students how to embrace failure and persist despite setbacks, what today we would call resilience or, as popularized by Angela Duckworth, "grit."[33] Before Duckworth, however, were Dewey, Montessori, Vygotzky, and Piaget, all of whom Papert embraced and drew inspiration from.[34]

What Papert did not embrace, however, were the educational scholars who wanted to research learning outcomes for students who had used Turtles or Logo. Following the success of *Mindstorms*, Logo and Turtles were widely adopted in schools. But Papert and his team did not conduct any educational research on the outcomes. Worse, those who did, including Roy Pea at Stanford and Tim O'Shea at the University of Edinburgh, found no substantive difference in learning gains between students who did and students who did not use the programs. In fact, what the students seemed to benefit from was the presence of a researcher who guided them through their learning with Logo.[35] Ironically, the students who took away the most from the computer did so because of the human interaction with the researcher, not the interaction with the computer.

Instead of modifying Logo or using these critiques to make it better, Papert "dug in his heels" and began disparaging "scientific" educational research involving treatment groups—the standard for most educational research.[36] In his 1987 essay "Information Technology and Education: Computer Criticism vs. Technocentric Thinking," he wrote, "It is a self-defeating parody of scientism to suppose that one could keep everything else, including the culture, constant while adding a serious computer presence to a learning environment. The 'treatment' methodology leads to a danger that all experiments with computers and learning will be seen as failures: either they are trivial because very little happened or they are 'unscientific' because something real did happen and too many factors changed at once."[37] Papert's assertion that Logo and computers could change a classroom's culture, and that the culture was responsible for better, or different, learning outcomes, is defensible. But this assertion, by his own admission, is unprovable. Ultimately, Papert's scholarly legacy in education was undone by his refusal to engage in the measurement techniques of the discipline, even as his ideas informed many educational practices and theories today.

Using Technology to Disrupt

Papert's idea of computers as elements of culture was rooted in the guiding principles of the now famous MIT Media Lab, which he helped found in 1985. The Media Lab grew out of Papert's Epistemology and Learning Research Group at the MIT Architecture Machine Group. MIT's website describes the goals of the lab in its earliest stages: "In its first decade (1985–1995), the Lab developed and demonstrated a wide range of ideas for how emerging technologies might transform learning, entertainment, and self-expression."[38] The diverse set of researchers brought together by the lab were homogeneous in at least one way, however. Like Papert, and like many at the institution, they were deeply rooted in the idea of hacker culture. Hacker culture at the time was based in a deep belief in the freedom of information, meritocracy, and the potential of computers to create a better world: "The themes raised again and again by hackers—free speech, meritocracy, privacy, the power of the individual—suggest that we can read the hacker material as a cultural case in which long-standing liberal ideals are reworked in the context of interaction with technical systems to create a diverse but related set of expressions concerning selfhood, property, privacy, labor, and creativity."[39] Papert wrote about his admiration for the playfulness of hacking and the themes of meritocracy and the power of the individual would inform his work for the rest of his life: "In particular, we have seen a strong alignment between constructionism and the 'hacker ethic,' and the deep convictions that gave rise to this ethos among the hacker community at MIT."[40] The hacker ethic reinforced the idea that Logo, with its learner-centric focus and egalitarian design could democratize education. It also reinforced the impossibility of Papert responding to criticisms from the "education establishment" on their own terms. The unwavering belief in Logo as an educational disrupter and the resistance to demonstrating educational outcomes informed all his future initiatives, including, in the turn of the century, the One Laptop per Child initiative, with mixed results.

Using Technology to Change the World: One Laptop per Child

"Build, code, play, rebuild, endlessly!"
—ADVERTISING COPY FOR LEGO MINDSTORMS

At the World Economic Forum at Davos 2006, Nicholas Negroponte, a faculty member at MIT, and cofounder, with Seymour Papert, of the MIT Media Lab, introduced his and Papert's newest project: One Laptop Per Child (OLPC). The idea was simple. The problems of poverty and lack of access to education could be partially solved by granting every child in the world an inexpensive laptop.

Papert had run a similar initiative in Maine, where he retired, and had also introduced giving laptops to incarcerated teenagers (boys) as well. Using Papert's experiments as a model, Negroponte introduced a grand vision for solving inequalities in, and lack of access to, "quality education" across the globe, particularly in areas where public schooling and the education of teachers was seen as substandard. The idea was that the laptop would provide an opportunity for students to teach themselves how to program, which built upon Papert's tightly held belief that programming a computer and debugging a program were the key to thinking about thinking, as well as a way to preserve childlike curiosity and encourage intellectual growth (at least the kind of intellectual growth that allows one to become a professor at MIT).

Inherent in this idea were several foundational assumptions that defined MIT's approach to educational technology in particular and presupposed the failure of these experiments to scale more broadly. Chief among these assumptions was that the ideal learner—a child—had all the characteristics and proclivities of what Morgan Ames calls the "technologically precocious boy."[41] The technologically precocious boy is someone like Papert himself, a boy fascinated by machines and motors and then by the computer—a child fascinated by engineering, by building things, by playing video games. These learners, besides being entranced by tools that were used for either construction or destruction, also did not need much guidance, were allergic to authority, and demonstrated a precocity for learning and experimentation that might be outside the norm. These characteristics were similar to those Suppes assigned to "gifted children" with several key differences, particularly the inclusion of women.

(Suppes's idea of giftedness was based in part on his own experience of those who were autodidactic and intellectually precocious, both male and female.) Decades later, MOOCs would base their appeal on providing access to bright children and adults to the so-called best courses (that is, courses from the world's most prestigious universities). EdX, for example, made much of the story of the one Mongolian teenager who attained a perfect score in a MOOC from MIT and ended up matriculating at the university the following year.[42]

But the vast majority of children who were given a laptop as part of the OLPC initiative used it as an entertainment device to watch videos and listen to music rather than as a way to construct knowledge.[43] A smaller percentage of students laptop did use the laptop as intended and received quantifiable educational benefits, although these students tended to be from families with higher socioeconomic status. However, the premise of OLPC (much like the premise of MOOCs five years later) was to enable higher educational equality across the globe. When introducing OpenCourseWare a few years earlier in 2002, MIT's own president, Chuck Vest, clearly expressed that access to education was not the same as providing an education. And in their analysis of OLPC, Mark Warschauer and Morgan Ames concluded, "Regrettably, there is no magic laptop that can solve the educational problems of the world's poor."[44] MIT's OpenCourseWare initiative, which was inspired by the principles of Papert, opened up course components (syllabi, readings, assignments) for free and was widely publicized.[45] This initiative, one of the more high-profile instances of Open Educational Resources, set the stage for the acceptance of MOOCs (which were initially free) by highly selective universities a decade later.[46] Yet MIT appeared to be ignoring its own history in OpenCourseWare when championing OLPC and edX.

Using Technology to Expand Access

At Stanford, Pat Suppes continued to experiment with developing sophisticated (for its time) educational software, which was distributed using CDs through his Education Program for Gifted Youth (EPGY). By the early 2000s, as connection speeds and quality increased, Suppes began using the new technology of the internet for web-based instructional programs and live virtual classes for high school students around the country and parts of the globe. Based on the success of these initiatives, he started the Online High School,[47] unbeknownst to many of the faculty and administration at the institution.

Pat Suppes officially retired from Stanford in 1992, just as his latest experiment in using computers in education, EPGY, was gaining momentum. His return to computer-assisted instruction was motivated by a request from the NSF. Suppes recalled, "But just before I retired in 1992, somebody came around from the NSF . . . and said, well you haven't been doing too much for us now in computers in education, why don't you do a calculus course on the computer?" Suppes led the development of an interactive calculus course that could be taught on the computer, and then began offering it to "very smart middle school students" in the local area. The appetite for advanced math courses in middle school and high school was strong—only a minority of high schools in the country offered calculus at that time, and Suppes saw a business opportunity in creating advanced math and physics courses for "gifted" middle and high school students who could not take these courses at their high school. Said Suppes, "And so by '92, the year that I retired, I decided to get back in this business at the university in a systematic way. We created the Education Program for Gifted Youth and then I went back into getting some grants for it."[48]

EPGY, as it was known, grew quickly. By 1996, the group had developed twenty-one courses (all distributed on CD-ROM) in secondary mathematics, Advanced Placement mathematics and physics, college-level mathematics and physics, and English language and expository writing courses. Suppes also created the EPGY's most successful product, a K–7 math course, which enabled students to move through the material at their own pace and then transition to the secondary mathematics courses (algebra and precalculus). All of the EPGY courses employed an algorithm that adapted the course content to the student's performance. (Suppes called this the "course motion.") First, the algorithm would conclude that a student had demonstrated "mastery" of course material, based on the accuracy of student responses, difficulty of the problem, and the topic. If the student had achieved mastery, the next course would be served to the student. If the student had not demonstrated mastery, a review would be given to the student along with a diagnostic.

By 2007, EPGY was a thriving business, serving thousands of students from about seven to seventeen years of age, and had expanded to include on-campus instruction through an initiative called the Summer Institutes. (These are still offered today under the banner of "Stanford Pre-Collegiate Studies.")[49] EPGY also had begun a series of English writing courses, which were taught primarily synchronously, over the internet, using voice and slides, combined with an asynchronous grammar course that was Stanford's first fully web-based, open-access instructional course. "So we're doing some of our most intense work in teaching English and using the computer. In fact, our most sophisticated use of the computer is in teaching English, because we are now writing big grammars that do the evaluation of grammar,"[50] said Suppes. (I was initially hired by Suppes to help write those grammars, aka potential instructor feedback that would be triggered by a student's actions in the courseware.) EPGY was one of the first initiatives to offer blended (in-person and online) education, taking advantage of the capabilities of the internet early on while also realizing the need for learners to gather in person when possible.

Stanford Online High School

In 2004, Suppes and the EPGY group received a grant from the Malone Foundation to expand its synchronous online writing courses to other subjects, and in a more formalized manner, by starting an Online High School (OHS).[51] Stanford OHS opened its virtual doors in 2006 with just a few dozen students, taking courses in grades 10–12. Early results were positive. OHS tapped into the needs of a previously underserved audience: academically advanced middle and high school students whose public schools did not offer advanced courses, and those students with strict external commitments (sports competitions, professional performances) that did not allow them to attend school regularly in person. The initial cohorts of OHS students enjoyed the experience, remained engaged in the virtual classroom, were accepted into prestigious colleges, and were able to thrive there. Based upon these results, OHS expanded in 2010 to include classes for grades 7–9.[52]

While the instruction and the students at OHS were advanced, the technology used to support a virtual school was not. The technological infrastructure was a weird admixture of existing platforms that coexisted uneasily at best. OHS used college.net for grading, Blackboard for the learning management system, Saba's Centra (in beta mode, which was constantly buggy) for the synchronous classroom, and study.net for readings. Teaching at the school in the early years required

FIGURE 5. The author in her Stanford office on OHS Pajama Day.

the ringleading skills of a circus master, managing unruly and early technologies, students with varying strengths of internet connection, not to mention a heterogeneous student body of varying physical ages, advanced cognitive abilities, and individual reasons for opting out of traditional schooling. As an English instructor of the younger students, I, along with my colleagues, was primarily concerned with keeping these thirteen- to fifteen-year-olds engaged, not only in our online classes but also in a virtual high school. We tried blended proms (both virtual and in-person), graduation ceremonies on Stanford's campus, virtual lunch hours, and all sorts of schoolwide theme days and peer social events to make students feel like they were part of a school community. The vast majority of our students graduated, and the OHS survived these early years to become one of the top ten private high schools in the United States.[53]

As the OHS grew and demanded more operational than academic expertise, Suppes turned his focus to neuroscience, focusing on what structural changes learning made to the brain. In a way, he had come full circle to the early days of McCarthy, Minsky, and Papert, and the earliest computer scientists, who were modeling the computer after the brain and trying to understand how learning worked in order to figure out how to teach the computer to learn. Suppes maintained that was still the wrong avenue: "I am skeptical of the earlier attempt to use digital computers as a model of the mind, a topic that is not so popular now, and with good reason." Suppes believed that his earlier predictions about the capabilities of computers to provide tutoring were premature and could only be achieved when humans could have "easy and natural" conversations with digital devices, saying, "I mistakenly and optimistically predicted in the 1960's . . . that in 30 or 40 years, computers would be doing the work of a modern Socrates in full-scale dialogue with students on nearly any subject they might choose. How foolish that was."[54]

EPGY and OHS were not the only online experiments at Stanford. The Engineering School offered an online master's degree in electrical engineering in 1998.[55] In 2005, Stanford became the first university to offer public access to campus lectures, concerts, and courses through iTunes U, with a reported fifty million downloads in the first seven years.[56] And John Mitchell, a professor of computer science, was building a better learning management system (LMS), called Courseware, that included machine-graded homework, "sophisticated" instructor dashboards, and discussion forums.[57]

Putting the Tech in Edtech

Big Tech was getting into the distribution of higher education as well. As content began to be understood as a way to attract consumer attention, which could be monetized (even though most of these business models were not fully developed yet), educational content was already online and was increasingly successful as a way to "attract eyeballs." Without a doubt, offering exclusive education for free aligned with the hacker mindset of the earliest web denizens. For Silicon Valley entrepreneurs, it would be a way for their business ventures to "save the world." Youtube.edu, iTunes U, and Khan Academy were all immensely popular, although they could be perceived as "additional noise in the marketplace" to learning management systems (LMSs) like Blackboard, according to Blackboard CEO Lou Pugliese.[58] The Open Educational Resource movement even inspired a new LMS, Canvas, to open-source its software. In the space of a decade, beginning in 2002, both educational content and the methods for delivering became free and easily accessible, in stark contrast to degree programs at elite universities, which were becoming increasingly exclusive in both price and admissions practices.

PART II

The Business of Higher Education

The rush of investment into technologies to help deliver higher education has shifted the language about the purpose of college to the same terms that measure the value of business. Current and prospective students consider the return on investment (ROI) of college in response to the rising cost and debt a degree now entails. To be sure, this is a marked change from the postwar twentieth century, when college was seen as a public good. But during the 1970s and 1980s, the way people in the United States thought about higher education changed. College was reframed as a private investment in the individual student—one that would pay off in increased earnings of more than a million dollars over a lifetime. This shift in thinking helped justify the shrinking of public funding for higher education and sharp increases in tuition that outpaced inflation. It also provided a basis for the privatization of student loans by 1992, which made more money than ever available to prospective students and their families and positioned higher education, and the loans that supported it, as an investment vehicle for banks and financiers. For-profit colleges became a significant business, one whose scale and profitability were enabled by the internet. Nonprofit universities also began to experiment with the internet as a way to reach learners and, in many cases, to create new sources of revenue. Few scholars or students thought to ask (as Richard Ohmann and Ira Shor did), "What happens inside the black box called 'college' that makes a difference in the job market and on through the following four decades?"[1]

Technological change and automation were thought to create increasingly complex work activities that required postsecondary education. In 2015, the Center for American Progress called for "College for All," predicting that "by 2020, 65 percent of all jobs will require bachelor's or associate's degrees or some other education beyond high school, particularly in the fastest growing occupations—science, technology, engineering, mathematics, health care, and community service." Their proposal included free community college and "support" for tuition and fees for public four-year institutions to be repaid according to income.[2] But just under ten years after this proposal, fewer students are enrolled in college, student loan debt is approaching $2 trillion, and a recent analysis shows that 45 percent of degree holders are underemployed a decade after graduation—that is, they are in roles that do not require a college degree.[3]

Nevertheless, during the 1990s and continuing through today, online education became a big business and then, during the Covid pandemic, the only business in higher education. More degrees from more universities were offered to anyone, anywhere with an internet connection. Some of these degrees were priced quite reasonably: the online MBA programs from University of Illinois and Boston University are offered for about $25,000 while the online master's in computer science

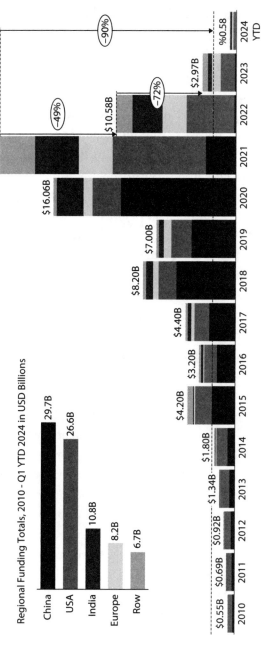

FIGURE 6. Holon IQ Ed Tech Funding Chart, April 1, 2024 from HolonIQ.com. *Source:* https://www.holoniq.com/notes/edtech-vc-collapse-at-580m-for-q1-not-even-an-ai-tailwind-could-hold-up-the-10-year-low.

from Georgia Tech is about $6,000.[4] Others were not: the online MBA from the University of North Carolina will cost learners over $125,000 while a master's in social work from the University of Southern California costs more than $100,000.[5] Notably, most of these programs were for those who had already completed a bachelor's degree; the number of students who earned a master's degree doubled between 2011 and 2021, corresponding with the rise in online degree programs.[6] In retrospect, it's perhaps not surprising that those who earned an undergraduate degree pursued a postgraduate degree; college had "paid off" for the majority of these learners, and the data showed that the more education you attained, the higher your salary was predicted to be.[7]

Universities were not the only entities profiting from online education. Edtech companies and those providing online program management services became a fertile area for private investment that grew dramatically before collapsing catastrophically a decade later. Thus, the same language used to frame college would align with the terms used to fund and operate a private enterprise. Built on the promise of the "college payoff," combined with the easy availability of federally subsidized student loans, current and prospective students were asked to consider the ROI of college for themselves, while universities were held to ever more comprehensive gainful employment rules "to protect hundreds of thousands of students from enrolling in programs that leave them with heavy debt loads, a worthless degree, and little in the way of career prospects."[8] To bring down individual costs and achieve even greater revenue, edtech companies like Coursera and edX, and online program managers like 2U, Wiley, and Academic Partnerships, talked about achieving "scale" (large numbers of students). The financial benefits of these scaled degrees delivered were obscured by the claim that they fulfilled a university's mission of providing access to education (without guaranteeing any outcome). The claim of access also permits edtech workers, university employees, and the students they serve to participate in a process that enriches already-wealthy institutions and investors without acknowledging that what they are doing is business as usual. The second half of this book will go inside the new private partnerships between edtech companies and universities to show the new realities (and business practices) that have created more access to higher education while at the same time reinforcing existing power structures and income disparity.

The increasing alignment between higher education, technology, and business has created a new phenomenon that may present a great threat to universities: certificates and other credentials from industry that fast-track a learner to employment. Google, IBM, Microsoft, Amazon, and others currently offer low-priced, easily available online education that is a much faster and cheaper way of making yourself employable than a two- or four-year degree. These programs have not been around long enough to compare the employment trajectory over time of learners who hold these kinds of certifications versus those who hold degrees (e.g., are they as well prepared as college graduates to flexibly adapt as scenarios and jobs change?), but the recent movement to remove degree requirements from job listings and for organizations to provide the kind of management training that allows for economic mobility without going to college, along with renewed interest in apprenticeships, indicates that the business of higher education may face real competition from industry in providing learners with education credentials that enable them to get jobs.

4

Learning Gets Managed and Monetized

And now look what they did with them: no longer are there computers in the hands of visionary teachers in the classrooms. The establishment pulls together and now they've got a computer classroom, there's a computer curriculum, and there's a special computer teacher. In other words, the computer has been thoroughly assimilated to the way you do things in school.
—SEYMOUR PAPERT, IN CONVERSATION WITH PAULO FREIRE, 1988

What's worth doing is worth doing for money.
—GORDON GEKKO, *WALL STREET*, 1987

Spreading the Higher Education Gospel on the Internet

The internet shared the same lineage as CAI and AI: developed by universities and aided by government funding and industry partnerships. First visualized at MIT in 1962 by J.C.R. Licklider (who then funded further research as head of computer science at DARPA), the internet was known as ARPANET in the 1970s and 1980s before Tim Berners-Lee invented the World Wide Web, which brought the technology to the masses in the 1990s.[1] Initially used by universities and government research centers to share computing power and data, the internet created networks over which information could flow instantaneously, transforming business, communication, human interaction, and, ultimately, higher education. The commercialization of the web in the 1990s and early 2000s would change higher education in a number of ways, all powered by the ability to both distribute educational programs and connect learners with instructors and each other. These new capabilities helped create the conditions for educational entrepreneurship, and many nonprofit institutions, particularly elite universities, tried to capitalize on the technology with a series of experiments designed to expand their influence and reach. Outside of academia, the transformative nature of the technology and its predicted effects on business, often referred to as the "knowledge economy," created a need for a more educated workforce. At the same time, the government removed limits on student loan borrowing, nominally to provide access to higher education, a move that accelerated the rise of for-profit universities as desirable investments in the private sector, as well as permitting nonprofit universities to raise tuition much faster than the inflation rate. The combination of new ways to distribute education, increased demand for that education, and easy access to loans to pay for that education would not only make higher education attractive to private investment but also accelerated the shift in public perception of higher education from a public good to a private investment in one's own earning potential, a shift that would create the conditions for investors to profit, for learners to become saddled with debt, and for a new technology to provide faster and cheaper alternatives to traditional higher education.[2]

In 1992, thirty-four years after the NDEA provided the basis for the federal student loan program, the Higher Education Act (HEA), originally passed in 1965, was up for reauthorization. Much had changed in the decades since the government first introduced student loans. Increased government funding, along with the introduction of federal student aid programs, led to a massive doubling of college enrollment: from five million in 1964 to nearly eleven million in 1975, largely driven by public universities and community colleges. However, by the 1980s, state funding for public universities was beginning to decline, leading to a rise in tuition costs that would ultimately far outpace inflation and an increased reliance on student loans for people seeking a college degree.

The 1992 HEA reauthorization responded to these changing conditions by expanding federal student loan programs, making it easier for families to borrow more money for college and enabling more students to attend. The growing demand for higher education was also seen as a profit opportunity by commercial banks and other lenders. Financiers lobbied Congress for policies that would not only use loans to expand higher education but also provide billions of dollars in subsidies to private lenders. They partnered with university leaders to advance their proposals, drawing on both alumni ties and client relationships with schools for whom they already had managed student lending at a smaller scale. Bankers presented themselves as coming to the rescue of colleges and students who were failed by a "centralized, federally administered program." The ready availability of these loans allowed states to withdraw support for higher education and incentivized universities to fill funding gaps by raising tuition. This expansion of federal student loans enabled public universities, which enroll over 62 percent of four-year degree seekers, to pay for rising enrollment demands with loan-financed tuition revenue. Borrowing for a college degree was seen as a smart investment for the individual and was certainly a great investment for the banks and investors who profited from the rising cost of college and the increased student debt burden for learners.[3]

As demand for higher education was increasing, so were the costs of attending a traditional nonprofit university. For-profit institutions, on the other hand, offered lower-priced educational programs online or in the evenings, flexibility that was valued by working adults. Because for-profit universities did not have tenured faculty with expensive employment contracts and fixed teaching loads, they were able to quickly respond to changes in market demand and offer courses in emerging fields. And unlike traditional universities, which rely heavily on government funding and donations, for-profit universities generated revenue primarily through tuition fees, making them less susceptible to fluctuations in public funding and more predictable in terms of revenue streams. As a result, private investors saw the for-profit education sector as a lucrative market with significant growth potential.[4]

For-profit universities grew rapidly in the 1990s and early 2000s, enabled by private investment and the ability to deliver instruction via the internet. In the period from 1970 to 2009, for-profit enrollment increased from 0.2 percent to 9.1 percent of total college enrollment. Not only were for-profit colleges the fastest-growing segment of higher education, they were also the most diverse by program and size, with the highest fraction of nontraditional students. Importantly, they also relied on federal student aid (loan and grant) programs for the greatest proportion of their total revenue.[5] And while both the internet and the relative affordability of personal computers fueled the expansion of for-profit colleges, so did the most maligned educational software of the time, the learning management system (LMS).

Managing Learning

In Andrew Molnar's 1969 report titled "U.S. Office of Education Support of Computer Activities," approximately 50 percent of the recorded expenditures were in support of computer-assisted instruction. The bulk of the remaining funds (35 percent) were spent on developing "Data Banks and Information Retrieval Systems" and "Computers in Administration and Organization."[6] Learning management systems were designed to administer and organize course materials as well as collect and store data on students. By the 1990s, the intellectual excitement about computers in education had been transformed into the grind of business. Computer-assisted instruction evolved into educational software, and many new players entered the edtech arena, including Microsoft, Mattel, and Broderbund.[7] Computers became smaller and more powerful, enabling the widespread use of computers in the classroom, as well as to store and manage school data. Learning management systems quickly became an integral part of education and a dominant force in educational technology.

In fact, for most schools, colleges, and universities, educational technology became nearly synonymous with learning management systems, which were about as exciting as they sound. Designed primarily for the management and support of course materials and grades, the LMS frustrated professors who wanted the systems to be more flexible. There were few alternatives in the market, however. By the early 2000s, no learning management system was bigger or more widespread than Blackboard.[8] In response, schools such as Stanford, the University of Maryland, and the University of Michigan began experimenting with creating their own learning management systems, sometimes called "courseware," that gave instructors more affordances for learning and experimentation than the traditional Blackboard. Through their tinkering, they combined elements of the LMS with components of CAI (automatic grading and real-time feedback on answers, peer connection) that would provide the design blueprint for MOOCs.

Blackboard's initial road map for success ultimately led to its downfall. Founded in 1994 by two college students, Michael Chasen and Matthew Pittinsky, Blackboard was the first LMS to be widely adopted by universities. Lou Pugliese, founding CEO of the company, describes the company's business plan as "grab as much real estate as you can. Become the embedded ERP (enterprise resource planning system)" and capitalize on the higher ed "we buy as a pack mentality." Pugliese would not be the last investor and CEO to exploit higher education's risk aversion to technology for their benefit; within the next two decades, many edtech companies would offer incentives and sweetheart deals to elite institutions to stimulate mass adoption. Besides being risk averse, universities are also reluctant to change, a characteristic Blackboard capitalized on by embedding itself into different components of a school's technology, including student records management. In other words, once you were on the Blackboard bus, it was difficult to get off. But Blackboard's strength in widespread adoption that reached deep into a university's infrastructure was also its weakness. Says Pugliese, "In our overzealousness—we ended up as a one size fits all experience—faculty had to adapt their teaching to the technology."[9] And by the late aughts, new open-source, customizable platforms were beginning to be adopted, particularly

Moodle, still popular twenty years later. However, during the early 2000s, Blackboard was the dominant LMS in the United States, and its restrictions encouraged a host of schools and entrepreneurs to experiment with new technologies to enable faculty to adopt their in-classroom teaching practices to online environments.[10] The widespread adoption of these (primarily for-profit) technologies and their increasing reach into schools and student experience did not go unnoticed by the federal government, which formed an office to help schools navigate the new education technology landscape.

1994: U.S. Office of Educational Technology

There shall be in the Department of Education an Office of Educational Technology (hereafter in this section referred to as the "Office"), to be administered by the Director of Educational Technology. The Director of Educational Technology shall report directly to the Secretary and shall perform such additional functions as the Secretary may prescribe.

—FROM THE U.S. CODE, 1994

The Office of Educational Technology (OET) was established to create guidelines for the use of educational technologies in schools. A "small but mighty office"[11] that technically reports to the secretary of education, OET is not focused on governance but instead encourages innovation in education and leverages their influence on grants made by the department.

One of OET's primary goals is to write a national educational technology plan that sets the agenda for educational technology.[12] This plan recommends software implementations and provides guiding principles as well as case studies for how technology can be deployed to increase access and to promote equitable practices. Although there is no requirement for states or districts to follow the plan, sometimes a state will adopt the plan wholesale, which can then guide its allocation of funds for educational spending. The plan is also important from a policy standpoint; it will serve as talking points for the secretary of education when discussing educational technology. The office, while small, can also have an outsize influence on grants through the Fund for the Improvement of Postsecondary Education (FIPSE). Spin-off projects include Quality Matters, Learners First, and a number of other initiatives, mostly at smaller (or community) colleges, to promote quality, equitable, and accessible teaching. While the Office of Educational Technology supports the use of edtech and some pilot innovations (educational blockchain, digital literacy),[13] the office can serve as a way for less resourced schools to take advantage of innovation in educational technology without being taken advantage of by profit-oriented edtech firms. On the other hand, well-resourced, elite universities can have much different relationships with educational technology, with some developing business models to gain market advantage by using new technologies to expand their influence and create additional sources of revenue, based on the successful business strategies of for-profit universities.

Another Gold Rush

The entrepreneurial opportunities for using the internet to distribute education benefited for-profit universities far more than nonprofits. Both types began exploring how to use the internet and e-commerce to try to create additional revenue streams, engage with new audiences, and provide value to their alumni. Enrollments in online degree programs from the less prestigious University of Phoenix skyrocketed, reaching 100,000 in 1999, five years after going public. Phoenix's revenues also grew at an astounding rate: "By the year 2000, Apollo stock had increased in value by 1,700 percent since its IPO. It was the nation's largest and fastest-growing private university, with operations in 35 states and a growing population of students from all over the world taking classes online."[14] The success of the University of Phoenix (and other for-profit universities operating almost entirely online) did cause the higher education industry to think more closely about online education as a source of revenue and brand expansion. A number of elite institutions began looking for ways to "monetize" their faculties' intellectual property and expand their influence by using the internet to reach new audiences. During this period, a number of for-profit ventures were launched by elite schools, including Fathom, an online effort led by Columbia University; All Learn, a concurrent initiative of Oxford, Princeton, Stanford, and Yale; and eCornell, NYUonline, and Virtual Temple.[15]

Fathom

"Distance-learning Ventures Propel Top Universities into For-Profit Sector: Harvard, Cornell, and Stanford among Those Lured by $10 Billion Potential"

—TITLE OF AN ARTICLE BY K. SINGER
IN *MATRIX: THE MAGAZINE FOR LEADERS
IN HIGHER EDUCATION*, 2000

In New York City, Columbia University was eager to successfully use the internet to leverage the intellectual capital of its faculty and those of similar institutions to develop non-tuition revenue streams. Columbia hired Michael Crow (now president of Arizona State University) to develop a plan for expanding access to Columbia's educational content. Incorporated as a for-profit company, Fathom launched in 2000 with ten partners, including two universities besides Columbia: the London School of Economics and the University of Chicago. Other partners were cultural institutions such as Cambridge University Press, the American Film Institute, the Smithsonian, and the British Museum.[16] Their initial focus was humanities courses. Their promotional materials indicated they offered over 600 courses that ranged in price from $50 to more than $500 and were fairly sophisticated in their design and delivery, combining multiple modalities for delivering instruction and enabling interaction: "The text-based courses were frequently enhanced by features like audio slideshows, animations, or interactive graphics, and some of the courses contained social networking elements like threaded discussions or moderated chats."[17] But although the product was new, the price was accessible, and the company received a decent amount of media attention, Fathom never broke even financially. Additionally, the faculty at Columbia were dismayed by the initiative and its lagging performance, and a university senate subcommittee on online learning and digital media initiatives launched an inquiry into Fathom. Shortly after President Lee Bollinger assumed office, in 2003, Fathom folded. Although Fathom was only in business for a short time, its failure cast a long shadow over elite institutions participating in for-profit, noncredit education online for the next decade, as did a similar venture from a subset of Columbia's peers.[18]

All Learn

In September 2000, in the midst of the dot-com crash, Stanford, Oxford, Princeton, and Yale invested a total of $12 million in a "distance learning venture to provide on-line courses in the arts and sciences to their combined 500,000 alumni."

All Learn, as the venture was named, was designed to bring the combined resources of the four-school alliance to their alumni because "the accelerating advance of knowledge is increasing the need for people all over the world to have access to lifelong learning. The spread of democracy and of market-based economies is expanding the number of people who want and would benefit from access to the finest teaching and information resources."[19] Led by Herbert M. Allison Jr., former president of Merrill Lynch, AllLearn.org was a "not-for-profit 501(c)(3) association governed by its member universities."[20] But the relationships among the four founding institutions soon soured. Princeton became disillusioned fairly early on, and Stanford and Oxford did not provide the financial support that Yale did. In fact, five years after All Learn launched, Yale was responsible for over half of the courses on the platform. Like Fathom, All Learn struggled to find "customers" (even their own alumni) who would pay for noncredit online courses; it ceased operations in 2006 due to unsustainable operating costs. And despite the partnership challenges, "the most common reason that leaders of both endeavors cite for the closures was a misunderstanding of customer behavior: namely, that there was not a sufficient market for fee-based online enrichment courses."[21] Yale's president during this time, Rick Levin, became convinced of the potential of online education; his experiences with All Learn would influence his decision to become CEO of Coursera in 2014 after retiring from Yale. However, when the dot-com bubble spectacularly burst in 2000, only two initiatives from elite universities in the United States found success in the next decade, and they did it by giving away their courses and courseware for free: MIT's OpenCourseWare and Carnegie Mellon's Open Learning Initiative.

Why MIT Decided to Give Away All Its Course Materials via the Internet

[Anyone] ... will ... be able to use the materials our professors rely on in teaching our full-time students. Together they will build a web of knowledge that will enhance human learning worldwide.[22]

—CHARLES VEST

In 1999, MIT was also exploring ways to participate in the new internet economy. True to standard academic operating procedure, a committee was formed: the Council on Educational Technology at MIT. One of the subgroups of this council was charged with "coming up with a project that would reach beyond the boundaries of our campus, beyond our classrooms."[23] Somewhat surprisingly, the committee decided that pursuing "MIT.com," a for-profit venture, was not desirable. However, the idea of using the internet to help spread education excited the committee members, particularly Dick Yue, associate dean of engineering, who came up with the idea of simply posting the course materials—readings, syllabi, assignment sets, and so forth—on the internet for free. President Charles Vest encouraged the development of this idea, and in 2001 OpenCourseWare was launched. The announcement provoked questions that continued to be asked a decade later, when MOOCs were introduced, including whether or not it was worth it to attend MIT now that the course materials were online and free. Vest addressed this question when he introduced the project, stating that "we are not providing an MIT education on the web. We are, however, providing core materials that are the infrastructure that undergirds that education. Real education, in our view, involves interaction between people. It's the interaction between faculty and students in our classrooms, in our living groups, in our laboratories that is the heart, the real essence of an MIT education. We think that, actually, OpenCourseWare will make it possible for our faculty and faculty in other residential universities to concentrate even more on the actual human process of teaching."[24]

Unlike the initiatives from Columbia, Yale, Princeton, Stanford, and others, OpenCourseWare was successful in expanding the influence of MIT through attracting new audiences of learners. Vest announced that the group would begin by creating a platform and putting 500 courses a year on the site; today, if you go to ocw.mit.edu, you will find the materials for over 2,500 courses, many of which have interactive components and instructional videos. You will also find comments and kudos from learners around the world who have used these courses to augment their education. OpenCourseWare has had a profound effect on learners worldwide. Unlike Logo and the MIT Media Lab's next project, One Laptop per Child, OpenCourseWare did not promise to disrupt the educational establishment, render teachers obsolete, or make money for the university. Said Vest at the press conference announcing the initiative, "When Andrew Carnegie decided he wanted to improve learning and quality of life across the United States, he didn't go out and found a for-profit correspondence school. He created a system of libraries. And I think that—I'd like to believe there's enough idealism and enough recognition that this really ought to be the bedrock use of the capability of the internet and the worldwide web and education." Vest's idea that the university should use the internet to distribute quality educational resources for free may have been counter to the idea of making a profit shared by other elite institutions, but it was not foreign to other universities in the United States and around the world.

Open Learning Initiative: Carnegie Mellon Marries Research and Practice

In 2002, Carnegie Mellon won a grant from the William and Flora Hewlett Foundation[25] to support the Open Learning Initiative (OLI), an open education initiative that provided free access to online courses. The courses at OLI were different from the OpenCourseWare at MIT because OLI involved faculty in a design process to completely reenvision their courses for web-based delivery, whereas OpenCourseWare simply provided access to a professor's teaching materials. This interdisciplinary approach drew on Carnegie Mellon's previous two decades of work of building on the ideas of computer-assisted instruction.

In the 1980s and 1990s, computer scientists and cognitive psychologists at Carnegie Mellon worked to create effective computer tutors (called intelligent tutors) that benefited students who used them.[26] Professor Ken Koedinger cofounded Carnegie Learning in 1983 as a research experiment that advanced the work of Suppes and Bitzer. Carnegie Learning was commercialized in 1998 and by 2008 was used in 7 percent of U.S. public school districts.

OLI had greater ambitions, however, aiming to make online education vastly accessible and highly effective by providing it for free. OLI was influential in its focus on evidence-based, computer-assisted learning in rich online environments. Studies conducted in the first six years of OLI found that students using OLI modules learned the same amount of material in a significantly shorter period of time with equal learning gains, compared to students in traditional instruction settings.[27] (A 2020 government report showed mixed results in academic achievement for students using OLI, although there were positive benefits in persistence and obtaining college credits.)[28] In the mid-2000s, however, the potential for free, effective online education to solve pressing social problems began to gain momentum, powered by a massively open university in the UK, significant charitable donations, and a UNESCO forum in Paris.

OER and Open University

First proposed in 1963 as "a University of the Air," Open University in the United Kingdom opened its virtual doors in 1971 with 25,000 students. Despite early challenges, including political resistance and cost overruns, by 2000 the Open University student body had grown to 190,000, half of whom were using the internet to connect to school. In 2006, it began making some of its courses available for free. And by 2021, over 2 million degrees had been awarded. Open University's ability to maintain quality instruction using innovative design principles and partnerships, including one with the BBC to produce and broadcast educational content, was an important proof point for educational technologists in the United States. Open University showed that distance education could be a quality education—at scale. Lou Pugliese calls it the "singular most important experiment in online learning," but one that does not get recognized often in the United States.

The success of OpenCourseWare and Open University also encouraged the Open Educational Resources (OER) movement. In 2002 UNESCO, in association with the William and Flora Hewlett Foundation and the Western Cooperative for Educational Telecommunications (WCET), convened the

Forum on the Impact of OpenCourseWare for Higher Education in Developing Countries. U.S. attendees from MIT, Carnegie Mellon, and the University of Texas, Austin met with representatives from universities in Africa and Asia who believed that open educational materials from universities in the United States would be valuable in providing greater access to advanced education, particularly in business, computer science, and health care.

UNESCO's report on the forum summarized a shift in thinking about higher education materials from a Western product to a property that could be shared globally: "Thanks to a confluence of technology and imagination, it is now feasible to recognize that knowledge as a social product can indeed become an international social property."[29] The principal financial backer of the open educational movement, the William and Flora Hewlett Foundation, would ultimately spend over $110 million by 2010 to support universities and other institutions in making their course materials free, with more than $14 million going to MIT.[30] The transformation of knowledge from a product held by a single university to a property shared across the globe was enticing to prestige universities, as it allowed them to participate in expanding access to their education at very little cost and without having to admit more students and potentially diminish their brand exclusivity. MIT, Carnegie Mellon and Open University showed that offering educational resources, including courses and adaptive tutors, did not "dilute" the university brand but rather enhanced it—without the reputational risk that for-profit ventures like Fathom and All -Learn carried. And free (or low cost) would become extremely attractive after the financial crisis of 2008 as more Americans struggled economically—in part because of the high cost of a college education.

Pricing Universities Out of Business

By 2012, student loan debt had surpassed credit card debt as the highest non-mortgage household debt. Pundits worried that a massive default in student loans would cause a collapse similar to the 2008 recession triggered by the housing market crash.[31] And while economists continue to crunch numbers and conclude that for the average person college does pay off in lifetime earnings, they also found that the 30–50 percent of students who don't complete college are worse off than if they had never attended, as they had lost earnings while in school and then were saddled with debt but no degree when they did enter the workforce. The combination of lost wages and lost income tax revenue for just one class entering college in 2002 and not completing a bachelor's degree by 2008 was calculated at $4.5 billion.[32]

Even economists who study college debt were sounding the alarm: "Nonetheless, despite the recent struggles of college graduates, investing in a college degree may be more important than ever before because those who fail to do so are falling further and further behind."[33] By 2011, a college degree appeared to be more necessary for individual economic security just as its cost seemed more burdensome than ever before. A strange dynamic was emerging in the higher education landscape: open online course materials and educational programs were becoming more prevalent, just as the sticker price for in-person education at nonprofit universities was reaching new heights. And at Stanford, a number of unconnected experiments in using technology to deliver education at a distance and to enhance the experience for students on campus were driving toward what some would call an "inflection point" in higher education.[34]

Working on the Farm

A couple blocks away from Pat Suppes's EPGY and OHS groups on the Stanford campus, a computer scientist named Andrew Ng was building a large neural network for Google X (the laboratory for Google) that by 2012 would be able to teach itself to recognize human bodies and cat faces.[35] At Stanford, Ng was also working on a side project to help make his popular machine learning course available to more students. Along with his fellow Stanford professors Jennifer Widom and Sebastian Thrun, Ng decided to "hack" John Mitchell's courseware project and build a platform that would allow anyone, anywhere in the world, to take one of his classes online. Unlike smaller classes, these had instructional videos tailored specifically to achieve learning objectives, automatically graded assessments, and peer interaction through forums.[36] In 2011 Ng, along with Thrun, a fellow computer science professor and Google employee, and Widom, chair of the computer science department, launched three separate courses, in machine learning, artificial intelligence, and database software, respectively, that were open to the public. The response was astounding. Buoyed in part by press in major outlets, the courses enrolled hundreds of thousands of learners from around the world in all "ages and stages" of life and learning. Forty thousand learners completed the courses, more than any of the three professors combined could hope to educate over the course of their lifetimes.[37] The Stanford online courses were MIT's OpenCourseWare brought to the next level; they put course content into platforms that simulated the experience of attending a large lecture with individual assignment feedback.

A few months after the surprising success of the Stanford courses, Sebastian Thrun, who was involved in developing

Google's self-driving car, announced he was leaving Stanford to launch a start-up, Udacity, that would offer free online courses that would help learners find jobs. The company raised $5 million from venture capital firm Charles River Ventures based on the idea that eventually, recruiters and corporations worldwide would pay to recruit from its pool of talented learners educated through their courses. Additionally, Udacity considered charging employers to offer continuing education to their workers.[38] Thrun claimed he was initially inspired to experiment with online education after hearing Sal Khan speak at the 2011 TED conference, where Thrun was presenting on Google's work with self-driving cars.[39]

Andrew Ng was also influenced by Sal Khan and Khan Academy but drew from a few different areas to create his online course platform: Mitchell's Courseware, Daphne Koller's practice of blended learning (or flipped classrooms), Gradience software, Lynda.com (now LinkedinLearning), and the community of StackOverflow. Four graduate students in Ng's lab, Jiquan Niam, Frank Chen, Chuan-Yu Foo, and Yifan Mai, cobbled together a platform based on Courseware and used it to offer Ng's course on machine learning and Widom's course on databases. These courses became the models for the first MOOCs of 2012. Although these courses were not explicitly designed using learning theory, both their design and technological affordances aligned with the principles of "andragogy" (i.e., adult learning) and employed many of the same cognitive-behavioral instruction methods as in-person programs, relying heavily on lecture-based instruction in which students demonstrate their learning through performance on a graded paper or exam.[40] What was different about these lectures and tests, however, was that the individual learner could watch and rewatch the lectures on her own time and at her own pace, which provided a new kind of access for learners who could not apprehend lecture material in the moment, for physical, geographic, or learning reasons.

The use of video lecture was championed at Stanford by Ng's colleague Daphne Koller, who recorded her standard lectures for students to view for homework—using class time to work on problem sets and interact with students to answer their question. Known as "flipping the classroom," this technique was attractive to professors who found themselves less inspired than they might like at the prospect of delivering the same lectures to students year after year. Students appreciated both the convenience and the more engaging classroom experience Koller's practice provided. And now, Ng's technology offered the ability not just to "flip the classroom" but also to open the classroom doors to the entire world. For the first time in the history of higher education, learners could take classes at name-brand institutions without leaving their homes or spending a dime. The idea of reaching a worldwide audience with their courses appealed to faculty, the idea of expanding access to their institution appealed to university administrators, and the idea of capturing millions of email addresses along with the attention of learners appealed to venture capitalists.[41]

In the Stanford tradition, Andrew Ng and Daphne Koller, whose husband was a successful tech entrepreneur, decided to pursue these open access online courses and form a company to explore making education available to anyone, anywhere, for free.

They called it Coursera.

5

MOOCs, 2012

July 2012, Mountain View,
California, 11:30 a.m.

Inside the third floor of a nondescript office building on El Camino Boulevard, Daphne Koller, a professor of computer science at Stanford University, MacArthur "genius grant" award winner, author of an influential textbook on probabilistic graphical models, and, recently, cofounder of Coursera, a startup that promised to use technology to massively scale education from the world's top universities, was running down a short hallway to a small office space crammed with three standing desks, four course operations specialists, and one large computer monitor displaying a free MOOC (Massive Open Online Course) on natural language processing. It was sixteen weeks after Coursera had launched and twelve weeks after *New York Times* columnist Thomas Friedman had written an op-ed that predicted a technology-enabled "revolution" coming for higher education, powered by platforms like Coursera and featuring a quote from Koller.[1] Coursera was offering just over a dozen MOOCs on the platform from the University of Pennsylvania, Princeton, Stanford, and the University of Michigan.[2]

Although the technology was in its early stages, Coursera was firmly in the crosshairs of national attention. Heralded as the much-needed technological disruptor for higher education, the start-up was staffed by a small team of young engineers and recent business school and college graduates that was frantically trying to keep up with platform-straining numbers of enrollments, demanding university partners, a white-hot glare of publicity, and impossible expectations. For Koller to even be in the office was unusual at this point: she was often flying across the world to meet with universities and speak at conferences. The speed with which she barreled down the hallway in her worn Birkenstocks gave the course ops team pause. Why was she interested in a MOOC that had recently ended, taught by one of her colleagues in Stanford's computer science department?

Koller stared at the screen. The natural language processing MOOC she was looking at was not hosted on Coursera's platform. It seemed to be hosted on Stanford's website.[3] The team watched her expectantly. Surely, she would be able to explain how Stanford was able to offer a MOOC? No one said a word. Koller was incredibly smart, direct, and quick to anger, and no one wanted to inadvertently light her fuse.

"Dammit," she said. The team manager, a twenty-four-year-old computer science graduate student named Pang Wei, rubbed his eyes and massaged his jaw. He nodded at Koller and the two of them left the room.

The remaining course ops team was puzzled. Why hadn't Koller been angrier? Oddly, she seemed spooked. There wasn't much time to hypothesize, as they were drowning in a flood of emails about the perceived deficiencies of the platform. Turning their attention back to electronically irritated university partners and frustrated learners, they assumed the company's biggest problem was that the codebase was still new and buggy, ill-equipped to withstand the number of users.

What the team didn't realize was that, technically, Stanford still owned Coursera's code.

Follow the Code

Computer code is a language that tells the computer what to do. Writing code can be like creating a recipe, and like a recipe, code goes through many drafts, getting refined each time. Also like a recipe, the basic ingredients of software code get developed first (the video plays, the quiz is graded, an email is generated) and then the aspects that delight the user—UX or user experience features—get developed later, after many iterations. Even though most omelets contain eggs, milk, and cheese, they do not all taste the same.

The initial code for the Coursera platform was created quickly to host a handful of pilot courses. The first software engineers were graduate students of Coursera's cofounders, Andrew Ng and Koller. Typically, start-ups get funding based on the promise of what their software *could* do; it's assumed that what the software *can* do is not ready for a full complement of users. Venture capital is supposed to be used to hire experienced engineers to create a fully functional, dependable, and user-friendly platform. But as interest in the initial MOOCs soared, and the publicity surrounding them rocketed into the stratosphere, there was not enough time to hire engineers to build out the platform out in a systematic, unified way. A few more experienced engineers joined Coursera's team early, but because of the popularity of MOOCs and the tremendous number of enrollees, there was no way to support a platform recode. The engineers worked overtime just to keep the platform from falling apart and were forced to create new functionalities without having time for full testing protocols. Time and capacity constraints hindered coordination, and different functions ended up being written in different languages. (A corollary would be trying to cook from a recipe written in English, French, and Slovakian.) It was a Frankensteinian codebase that was never intended to support the massive scale of the first MOOCs.

Also, in partnership with universities, the team was making up this new form of education as they went along and inadvertently creating more problems for the overstretched and inexperienced engineers. Beyond Andrew Ng's early course the previous year, there were few templates or examples of what a Massive Open Online Course was, and so university partners defaulted to designing courses that mimicked traditional college courses: twelve to fourteen weeks long, with one to two hours of lecture videos each week. Initially, the course content was "gated," meaning that new lectures and assignments opened—or dropped—each week at midnight on Sunday. This timing was a self-inflicted wound of the highest degree as it created the conditions for a heavy influx of users on the platform every Sunday night. The database and software could not support the load. On Monday mornings, nearly half of the employees would cram into the engineers' office (a conference room repurposed to hold eight workstations) and look at the latency reports—a display of how long it takes for the platform to respond to a user request. Even to an untrained eye, it was easy to see the platform was straining to keep up. The graph looked like an EKG of someone having a heart attack, with high peaks and valleys and then a dip and flatline.

The instability of the platform was not the only issue that needed attention. Prestigious, R1 (Research 1 universities) were calling Koller and Ng in a rush to partner with Coursera and "get online." In early June 2012, the president of the University of Virginia (UVA), Theresa Sullivan, was forced to resign her position after Helen Dragas, head of UVA's board, argued that "Virginia was falling behind competitors, like Harvard and Stanford, especially in the development of online courses, a potentially transformative innovation."[4] Although Sullivan was shortly reinstated, university presidents across the country took notice and called Coursera to see if they could offer courses through the platform to "check the box" of online educational innovation. Coursera's funders, the well-known and deep-pocketed venture firms Kleiner Perkins and New Enterprise Associates, were delighted by the momentum. Even though neither Coursera's staff nor the code could support the volume, the investors encouraged more growth. While Ng and Koller continued meeting with universities to discuss partnerships, and the staff and engineers kept the platform running through twenty-hour days of software bug fixing and human intervention, plans were being made to rewrite the code as soon as humanly possible. Because the code was developed by Stanford students and professors, legally, Coursera's code was owned by Stanford. And the process for transferring that code from Stanford to Coursera had not been completed.

The Office of Technology Licensing

Inventions of Stanford faculty, students, and staff are owned by the university. The idea is that the role of the university is to produce knowledge through faculty research and the work product of staff and students, which it pays for in the form of salaries, facilities, grants, and other types of support. If a Stanford invention is deemed to be commercially viable, however, then the university's Office of Technology Licensing will "license them to industry." That industry could be an external corporation, a start-up founder, even the professor herself. Typically, the university licenses the majority of the shares of the invention to the inventor or, in the case of industry, the purchaser, retaining only a small portion for the university. Once Koller and Ng knew that venture capital funding for Coursera was imminent (likely early spring 2012),[5] they should have begun the process of transferring ownership of the code from Stanford to Coursera, following in the footsteps of Larry Page and Sergey Brin (Google), Jerry Yang (Yahoo), and others. The Office of Technology Licensing handles the paperwork and the distribution of any revenues to those who may have contributed to the original idea and uses its own share of the "cash royalties" as unrestricted funds, which are reinvested in the university. This has proven to be a lucrative business model for the university: in 2023, Stanford received over $59 million in licensing revenue from more than 1,000 technologies (although only 6 generated a million dollars or more).[6]

In the case of a start-up, where investors are betting money that a Stanford idea can be monetized, Stanford takes, as payment, the right to invest in future financing rounds. For example, the collaborative, social MOOC platform NovoEd was licensed from Stanford to its inventors, Farnaz Ronaghi and Amin Saberi. As payment for its investment in developing the ideas that resulted in NovoEd, Stanford reserved the right to invest in the company's first round of funding, called a Series A, which is usually led by venture capital firms. This approach, although riskier than a royalty agreement, can be astonishingly lucrative when the bet pays off: Google, Yahoo, and Tableau are all Stanford inventions.[7]

Coursera, too, seemed to be poised for takeoff. Within its first six months, the company grew from four university partners to thirty-three, from two MOOCs to two hundred, and from two hundred thousand users to two million. One would assume Stanford would be eager to retain the option to own some of the company. But in those six months, Koller and Ng had not yet begun the process of licensing the technology from Stanford to Coursera. And Stanford, as it turned out, had only agreed to let Coursera host Stanford courses just once.[8] It appeared both parties were playing a game of "intellectual property chicken" with Coursera frantically rewriting the codebase to make it an invention of Coursera and not of Stanford.

Clearly, Stanford was tired of waiting. The university exercised its right to claw back the code, which it did—not by taking legal action against Coursera but by using a copy of the code to create its own platform, called Class2Go, and offering Stanford MOOCs on that platform instead of Coursera's.[9] What Koller was looking at in the office in July was the beta version of Class2Go. What she did not know was that other universities, troubled by the for-profit designation of Coursera, and looking for a nonprofit alternative, began asking Stanford to host their own courses.

Koller was distressed. Coursera was growing rapidly, but Stanford was one of the tentpole partners and lent critical credibility to not just the platform but also the idea of Massive Open Online Courses. Just one month after Coursera's official launch in April, Harvard and MIT announced their own MOOC platform, edX.[10] While MIT had a long history of open courseware, the university was a few months behind Stanford in offering MOOCs. Following the success of the first MOOCs in the summer of 2011, Piotr Mitros, an MIT PhD and software engineer wrote to MIT president Rafael Reif and let him know that Sebastian Thrun was flying him out to California to help rewrite the code for Udacity's platform. Reif ultimately hired Mitros as a research scientist and gave him the resources to create a scalable online course platform called MITx. In February 2102, the first MITx course, featuring professor Anant Agarwal, was offered to MIT students. In March, Reif funded the initiative with $5 million. Coursera was moving faster, however, and was getting more media attention.

In order to compete, Harvard and MIT put up $30 million each to transform MITx into edX and appointed Agarwal, director of MIT's Computer Science and Artificial Intelligence Laboratory (which evolved from Minsky and Papert's Artificial Intelligence Laboratory), as CEO of the new venture.

By September, Stanford formally announced Class2Go as an alternative to Coursera and edX. In just four short months, Coursera went from owning the MOOC category and blowing past Udacity to having two more competitors, backed by arguably the three biggest university brands in the country. It appeared Coursera's initial takeoff velocity would be slowed by both market forces and university partner pushback.

Clash of the Titans

Every start-up has an "origin story" and they are almost always partial truths. Coursera's origin story was that Koller invited a few venture capital friends over for brunch one spring afternoon and went to sleep that evening having secured $16.5 million in Series A funding from Kleiner Perkins and New Enterprise Associates.

What also happened was that Stanford had established a committee in 2011 to think through the implications of online education for Stanford and for higher education. The group met at Gates Library (in Stanford's Computer Science Building) and included various stakeholders at Stanford—professors, deans, and administrators who were involved in Stanford online experiments both big and small: Pat Suppes's Online High School and Education Program for Gifted Youth, the School of Engineering's online master's programs offered through Stanford's Center for Professional Development (SCPD), iTunes U, and others. Additionally, the university commissioned a report on the state of online learning at Stanford to be presented at the faculty senate in April 2012. In that report, the provost, John Etchemendy, compared the internet to the printing press in terms of its effect on spreading education. "The printed book transformed higher education, including the efficiency with which knowledge could be disseminated. The question is—can digital technology have a similar effect on education, on higher education?" he asked.[11]

Outlining the business practices of universities against a wider economic backdrop, Etchemendy defined the university as a service industry, with highly educated service providers who were hard to find and hire and whose services were impossible to scale without a corresponding decline in quality. Etchemendy's argument was both elegant and humorous—he compared the business models of dentistry and university and found them identical. His core argument left little room for debate about the pressures facing higher education and the potential for technology to radically change the cost of doing business—educating college students. Possibly, the provost had been practicing his point of view for a few months at least. Earlier that spring, he hosted a yearly meeting of provosts from the Ivy League, Michigan, Berkeley, and Chicago (the Ivy Plus). In conversations during and after that meeting, Etchemendy, known as "Etch," persuaded three provosts to join Stanford in backing a homegrown technology developed by two of its computer scientists, Daphne Koller and Andrew Ng. Those provosts—Christopher Eisgruber of Princeton, Martha Pollack of the University of Michigan, and Vincent Price of the University of Pennsylvania—went back to their respective campuses and announced that their institutions would be participating in this new form of education: Massive Open Online Courses. This move would be highly beneficial for each of their careers. Price would become the president of Duke, Pollack the president of Cornell, and Eisgruber the president of Princeton. In retrospect, it is easy to see why Etchemendy would be able to advocate for higher ed embracing technology as a transformative force rather than just a managerial one.

Stanford was making a significant effort to set Coursera up for success—recruiting its first university partners, or suppliers, to help make its products: MOOCs. Now Coursera needed the money and business guidance to operationalize the production of the products, sell them, and scale the business. Obtaining funding was just one part of the puzzle—getting the right set of advisors to help guide the business was another, more critical piece. Harvard and MIT "self-funded" edX with a combined initial investment of $60 million.[12] Stanford clearly had the money to do the same with Coursera. But John Hennessy, Stanford's president, knew that obtaining funding for Coursera was the easy part—there were many venture firms and individuals who could write a check for a few million to get the company off the ground. The scarcer and more valuable resource was the know-how and expertise for guiding the business and product to be scalable. Although Stanford did not invest money in Coursera initially, the institution played a significant role in helping the company get the right guiding hands to make it a success. In addition to being Stanford's president, John Hennessy was also a director at two venture capital firms: Kleiner Perkins and Foundation Capital. Kleiner Perkins (KP) led the Series A round for Coursera, and John Doerr, KP's chairman, became a recognizable face in Coursera's hallways.[13]

The Invisible Hand

John Doerr is a legend in Silicon Valley. An early investor in Sun Microsystems, Google, Twitter, Uber, and others, Doerr preaches the gospel of "measuring what matters" to achieve results (his book, *Measure What Matters*, goes deeper on the topic). Doerr is less of a dreamer than a doer, believing firmly that big ideas are easier to come by than the great execution necessary to make them successful. His development of Intel's system of performance measurement, Objectives and Key Results (OKR), has spawned Key Performance Indicators (KPIs) at Google and others and is widely influential across businesses. A practical-minded investor, Doerr visited Coursera in the summer of 2012 a few times and was actively advising its growth.

A key aspect of Doerr's advice on execution and measurement was "building to scale." Scaling is a synonym for growing an organization or enterprise in a manner that reduces waste and increases efficiency and, thus, profitability. In a start-up, creating practices and processes that scale most often means automating tasks whenever possible, then encouraging the user to do those tasks for themselves (i.e., changing your email address on your account yourself) and only using human capital (in Coursera's case, staff and engineer time) as a last resort. Doerr also preached the gospel of focusing on the end user of the platform, not on the competition, nor on the many university complaints we staff received about the platform. "The learners are our customers," Ng would remind the team, again and again, as they fielded angry emails about the platform from partner universities. Although focusing on the learners was the right move for the business, it created a season of hell for the course operations staff, who were trying to keep universities happy while also trying not to distract engineers with bug fixes or requests for improvements.

This tension resulted in comical (now, although not at the time) situations where the four course operations specialists were performing a kind of triage on the platform to make it appear more functional than it was. Case in point: peer-review functionality, the "killer feature" of the Coursera platform, designed to allow the teaching of humanities, writing, art, and other creative courses (including software development), was written in a computer language separate from the rest of the platform and had no user interface. Practically, this meant that when a peer review was enabled in a course and an instructor wanted to change due dates or the number of peer reviews a learner had to complete before seeing their own feedback, a course operations specialist had to go "in the back end" (into the raw code) and make the changes as the course was live. This process is roughly the equivalent of performing an oil change while your car is traveling down the highway at eighty miles an hour—dangerous to do, but less dangerous than doing without.

On the other coast, edX may not have had John Doerr, but the company did have access to MIT's robust alumni network of successful entrepreneurs as well as design and computer science pioneers such as Joi Ito and Hal Abelson (who wrote the user manual for Logo and directed OpenCourseWare).[14] EdX positioned itself as the "academically oriented" nonprofit alternative to Coursera's venture capital–backed business model.[15] But after an initial boost in gaining partnerships with schools

FIGURE 7. The author (second from right, in the front of the image) at Coursera, 2012. "Coursera team, 2012" from John Doerr, *Measure What Matters: How Google, Bono, and Gates Foundation Rock the World with OKRS* copyright © 2018 Bennett Group LLC. Used by permission of Portfolio, an imprint of Penguin Publishing Group, a division of Penguin Random House LLC. All rights reserved.

that had once been exclusive to Coursera, edX would ultimately offer fewer courses from fewer universities and attract fewer learners.[16] Coursera's "scale fast" ethos had a powerful proponent in Stanford's president John Hennessy, whose own professional background was steeped in the mindsets and practices of Silicon Valley.

Founding Father

John Hennessy was unusual for a college president in his active ties to industry and finance, in addition to being a highly reputable scholar and administrator. As a professor, he took a year sabbatical to become CEO of a tech company that was sold for $330 million (in 1990 dollars) and, once he became president of the university, also spent significant time working for the Stanford Fund to learn the ins and outs of managing the endowment. (All universities with a sizable endowment have an entity that manages the institution's portfolio.) Hennessy was fascinated by the flow of money between industry and Stanford, particularly how this relationship converted a professor's intellectual property (IP) into cash.[17] Because universities are nonprofit, they have to sell their shares in any company once it goes public—at which point the Stanford Endowment purchases those shares so Stanford can benefit from the market while still maintaining its nonprofit status. It is an elegant and highly profitable solution to the problem of retaining faculty and monetizing their output.

While intellectual property rights and trademark may not seem to be a critical linchpin of a university's success, the process of "licensing out" intellectual property played a significant role in Stanford's transformation from a regional school to a global leader in innovation. Through the early and mid-twentieth century, MIT was seen as the nation's university leader in technological innovation. Like Illinois, they derived a noteworthy revenue stream from Defense Department contracts that capitalized on faculty knowledge and research. In Palo Alto, Professor Frederick Terman, former director of the Harvard Radio Research Lab, which was responsible for U.S. electronic warfare in World War II, became dean of Stanford's engineering school in 1944 and then provost in 1955, and played a significant role in attracting federal contracts and fostering entrepreneurship. He used his relationships in Washington to secure federal contracts for university labs and local firms, which directly benefited Stanford's research and development programs. He also introduced three institutional innovations during the 1950s: first, establishing the Stanford Research Institute (SRI) to conduct defense-related research and assist West Coast businesses, and second, promoting the development of the Stanford Industrial Park, which attracted companies such as GE, Eastman Kodak, and Hewlett Packard (founded by Terman's students William Hewlett and David Packard). The third innovation was the Stanford Instructional Television Network, which allowed engineers at electronics companies to attend graduate courses without having to leave work. Each of these innovations blurred the boundaries between the campus and the technology firms surrounding it. Many of those same firms produced successful entrepreneurs who reinvested their earnings in promising new companies, and by 1974, the region was home to more than 150 active venture capitalists.[18]

Five decades later, John Hennessy also became the dean of engineering and then provost at Stanford. Steeped in Terman's model of the free flow of ideas from university to industry, Hennessy served as both an advisor to and investor in two venture capital firms, Kleiner Perkins and Foundation Capital. By scouting ideas on "The Farm" and bringing them to the attention of venture capital, Hennessy profited personally from multiple inventions during his tenure, including Google, Yahoo, and Netscape.[19] In 2012, Coursera was just the latest Stanford start-up that had gotten a leg up on financing and advising from Hennessy.

MIT, on the other hand (and coast), was not about to be overtaken by Stanford again, not with educational technology. Sure, Stanford had Pat Suppes and other experiments in education technology, but MIT had its own legacy of experimentation, crystallizing with Seymour Papert and then moving forward with OpenCourseWare and the One Laptop initiative. Just like Coursera, edX suddenly had to bear the weight of unanticipated participant load (although edX's codebase was initially far more stable than Coursera's). While Andrew Ng, Daphne Koller, and edX's Anant Agarwal criss-crossed the country talking about the technology that would disrupt higher education for good,[20] back in Mountain View, a handful of doctoral students were writing code to support a rapidly increasing audience. Although Agarwal, Koller, and Ng were each recognized as successful academics, in 2012 their MOOC hype was far more successful than their MOOC platforms.[21] And with every new university that signed with Coursera and edX, and every news story that teased the coming disruption of higher ed, a storm was brewing that threatened to crush Coursera's fragile codebase.

Surfing the Tsunami

It wasn't just the popular news cycle. Higher ed was intent upon disrupting itself. When Stanford and Hennessy were profiled in 2012 in the *New Yorker*, the article, "Get Rich U.," concluded with a quote from Hennessy about distance, or online, education: "There's a tsunami coming." Hennessy would use this metaphor consistently over the next few years as a raison d'être for participating in online education, at scale, and right now.[22] Although the rapid adoption of MOOCs may have appeared to be both hasty and uninformed, in reality, the conditions for producing a higher ed tsunami had been an open secret for at least a decade. Rising tuition prices combined with lower household income after the 2008 financial crisis caused students to borrow more money for college. By 2012, total student loan debt was approaching the trillion-dollar mark, and the cost of higher ed was called into question.[23] Well-known academics and administrators such as William Bowen, Robert Archibald, and David Feldman had been writing and speaking about the inability of traditional higher education to meet the needs of society for a more educated workforce without tremendous financial investment, a time when the burden of paying for a college degree shifted from the government to the students and their families.[24]

During this period, the former president of Princeton, former president of the Andrew W. Mellon Foundation, and influential author and educator William G. Bowen began publishing a series of essays on the "cost disease" of higher education. Bowen described it this way: "In labor-intensive industries such as the performing arts and education, there is less opportunity than in other sectors to increase productivity by, for example, substituting capital for labor. Yet, over time, markets dictate that wages for comparably qualified individuals have to increase at roughly the same rate in all industries. As a result, unit labor costs must be expected to rise relatively faster in the performing arts and education than in the economy overall."[25] In short, Bowen argued, educating students is a time-intensive task performed by highly trained, expensive labor (teachers and professors) and therefore is relatively immune to traditional cost-saving measures, particularly automation or digitization.

Bowen had first applied cost disease theory to higher education in 1968, in a study published by the Carnegie Commission on Higher Education. As part of the prominent annual Tanner Lectures at Stanford in 2012, just as MOOCs were gaining widespread attention, Bowen's lectures, titled "The Cost-Disease in Higher Education: Is Technology the Answer?" brought together several ideas about the current "crises" in higher education, including lower four-year completion rates, widening achievement gaps between wealthy and poor children, and the financial instability of many colleges and universities, which produce higher tuition rates, which in turn produce a rising sense of distrust in, if not disgust with, higher education itself. As Bowen said, "No part of higher education is immune from the consequences of ignoring this rising tide of anger and resentment."[26]

For Bowen, improving quality and access and decelerating costs were of paramount importance if the university was to survive. Technology offered a way to achieve these goals. He said: "I continue to believe that the potential for online learning to help reduce costs without adversely affecting educational outcomes is very real." In 2012, he predicted today's "crisis of confidence" in the value of higher education, adding, "We must recognize that if higher education does not begin to slow the rate of increase in college costs, our nation's higher education system will lose the public support on which it so heavily depends."[27]

In an incredible confluence of timing and location, Bowen sounded the alarm about higher ed pricing itself out of business to a crowded auditorium of people who could get rich by developing the solution. Technologically delivered education was a way to scale faculty members and increase access to higher education. Presidents, provosts, faculty members, staff, edtech entrepreneurs, and venture capitalists (sometimes all in the same person) were drunk on the idea of solving this societal ill and the recognition and potential fortune that would come with addressing it.

Just as importantly, Bowen's challenge was a blessing from the old school Ivy League to the new school of online education. Previously a second-class citizen of education, "online ed" was now new and sexy. One prevailing thought was that "old" online education—that is, traditional distance education—was a relic of Web 1.0: the idea of internet as access. But 2010–13, which saw the unimaginable popularity of Facebook, Twitter, and Instagram, was Web 2.0—the idea of the internet connecting people, or the social web. A few popularly held assumptions swirled around each other with enough velocity to create a perfect storm for "the great disruption of higher education." In 2008, Harvard professor Clayton Christensen wrote *Disrupting Class: How Disruptive Innovation Will Change the Way the World Learns*, which argued that technology can play a crucial role in delivering personalized education, allowing students to learn at their own pace and receive tailored instruction. Christenson suggested that adaptive software and online platforms can act as virtual tutors, providing individualized feedback, adapting to the student's progress, and offering customized learning experiences. This technological disruption, which had been designed, developed, and distributed by Suppes and Bitzer forty years earlier, was meant to be the solution for education that was relevant to careers, since "what American students most need are the tools and skills that will help them compete for the increasingly sophisticated jobs of tomorrow."[28]

Bowen's embrace of technology and Christensen's call for disrupting education echoed across a nation that was using computers and mobile phones to amplify connectivity. Social media was becoming more popular. In 2011, Arab Spring swept across the Middle East, enabled by Facebook and Twitter. In 2012, Facebook went public. Instagram was purchased for a billion dollars (by Facebook). In Palo Alto, as home prices soared and twenty-three-year-old engineers who had been working full-time for about twelve months were putting in orders for their new Teslas, a fever of "what's next" gripped Silicon Valley. Into this mix were technology platforms developed at Stanford (Coursera and Udacity) and MIT (edX), the tacit blessing of Harvard, Princeton, the University of Pennsylvania, and the University of Michigan, and funding from one of the most successful venture capital firms in the world, which had also bet on Amazon and Google. The conditions were perfect for Hennessy's tsunami to start. The story had already been written in the public imagination when the press took it up. The first crest of the wave was Tom Friedman's May 15, 2012, article in which he summed up the argument for a massive disruption of the American higher education system and gave his blessing for Massive Open Online Courses to "Let the revolution begin."[29] Now the ideas of academics and university presidents were summed up neatly by the *New York Times'* most widely read columnists. The revolution was going to commence, and quickly.

Which at the ground floor—or the industrial carpets of Coursera's rented home office—meant there was no stealth mode to perfect the code and build the functionalities necessary to do what Coursera was seen as promising to do: provide a world-class education to anyone in the world, for free. For a start-up, the only thing worse than having no customers for your product is having too many customers too soon. The consequences for creating bad word of mouth about your product at scale are that no one is likely to use it again. And the company was laughably underresourced. In late June 2012, there were just twenty team members servicing four university partners (I joined the course operations team during this period). Four weeks later, Coursera announced twelve more university partners and had grown the team to about twenty-five employees.[30] Each new university partner meant new courses with enrollments in the tens, if not hundreds, of thousands. Meanwhile, the team was busy doing all the things a start-up in its earliest stages should be doing: making sure the code worked, that it was written clearly and well, that the database could handle the traffic.

Rapid growth is catnip to investors, and the press were climbing all over themselves to report on higher education's revolution. The *New York Times* declared 2012 the "Year of the MOOC."[31] In the space of a few weeks, Thomas Friedman, Peter Norvig (head of education from Google and co-instructor of one of the first MOOCs), and various university deans, provosts, and professors came to lunch in Coursera's conference room with Koller, Ng, and the young team. The globe had contracted "MOOC fever." This form of education, which wasn't even yet a year old, was seen as the solution to poverty, social unrest, extending life expectancy, the doctor shortage, the nursing shortage, the computer-programmer shortage, and the teacher shortage, all the while creating a shortage of rational thinking about what a technology could reasonably do, while inducing a collective amnesia about any educational technologies of the past.

Meanwhile, Koller continued to sign university partners faster than the company could possibly service them in an ultimately successful attempt to become bigger than edX and Udacity. Back at the home office, the course operations team (myself, a postdoc in computational biology, a recent Stanford history graduate, and one of Koller's advisees) was so sleep-deprived and brain-fogged it was impossible to see beyond the crush of emails and urgent code fixes and to even imagine ever answering or addressing them all. Koller kept the names of the university partners she was in negotiations with on a spreadsheet that she showed the team during daily group lunches. What she did not show was the second sheet of all those who were calling and trying to partner with Coursera. The handful of course operations specialists—who were bridging the gap between the patched codebase and the user—were beyond overwhelmed and overworked. A sort of battle fatigue set in. Once you assumed that you would only sleep five hours a night, that there would be at least one senior leader from a name-brand university infuriated with you and demanding answers, that you would never ever be able to provide accurate and satisfactory solutions, that you would eat standing up at your desk, that the code would break, that you would make mistakes because you were so tired, and that the next day would be exactly like the last one, it was sort of okay.

Koller and Ng did understand the problem. But their hands were tied. They had to make the codebase more solid, less prone to error, and also not owned by Stanford. All financial resources went into shoring up the engineering ranks. The course operations specialists were trained in html to handle the low-level code requests from partners. For instance, even someone without any formal computer science training (such as myself) became adept at going into "the back end" of an assignment to change the code so that it would work the way professors intended. Regardless of position or role, everyone at the company was working impossible hours against a backdrop of intense press hype and heightened hysteria from the highly optics-sensitive universities who were Coursera's early partners.

When in Doubt, Optimize

In an attempt to ease the workload and optimize performance of the "humans in the loop"—the course operations team—Ng devised an experiment. One day, he arranged for the entire team to answer emails together in one office with their computers linked to a timer. For eight hours, as they answered emails, they categorized each as being either technical support, course design support, or emotional support—those emails smoothing the ruffled feathers of professors or university leaders. Each member of the team was ranked by how quickly emails were answered. Group response times were sorted to see how time-consuming each category could be. The conclusion was that individual emails were an inefficient way to provide support to university partners and that the course operations function was an impediment to scaling the number of learners and courses on the platform.

The solution to this problem was "docs"—a set of standardized responses to common questions that would serve as a self-help resource for universities. The problem with the solution was that technical documentation writing is more time intensive than it may seem, and Ng became frustrated by the amount of time it took. He assumed that once someone answered a common question via email then that same email could be copied and pasted into a doc. He was not wrong—that process is necessary for the first stages of documentation. But what neither he nor the rest of the group knew was that it was not sufficient for creating a self-help database of Frequently

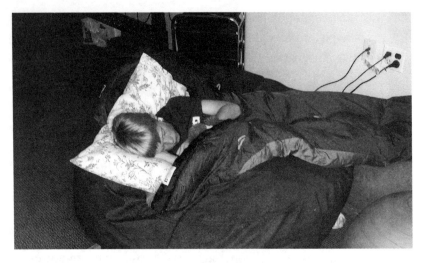

FIGURE 8. The author's son during an all-nighter.

Asked Questions. And because the technology enabled teaching and learning at a scale no one had previously been able to achieve, problems and questions were being created faster than solutions and answers.

MOOC frenzy intensified through the fall of 2012 and the pace of work was relentless. In July 2012, Coursera signed twelve more partners. In September of that year, the company had signed sixteen more.[32]

Different Time Zone, Different Business Model

EdX too was making strides but with a very different business model. Initially, edX invited partners to join its platform in return for an investment. EdX promised to produce courses and provide research opportunities for university partners. Their pitch was that they were "of the university" and therefore much better qualified to offer educational technology than the for-profit Coursera. EdX was growing more slowly than Coursera, in part because of their commitment to the quality of the codebase and because they had time to create some in-depth computer science and technical courses that pushed the boundaries of what kind of rigorous online education was available to the public at scale. At the start, edX was wholly consistent with MIT's perspective on higher education: the first MOOCs were built upon the foundational values of MIT OpenCourseWare, so much so that edX announced its intentions to make its code open source. EdX was being positioned as the nonprofit counterpart to the venture-backed Coursera, capitalizing on the wariness with which universities perceived Stanford, which by 2011 had roots in 39,900 active companies. (If these companies collectively formed an independent nation, its estimated economy would be the world's tenth largest.)[33] The perception of edX and MIT as being less focused on profits than Coursera and Stanford was a masterful sleight of hand, given that edX would ultimately provide a handsome return to both institutions and MIT's influence on business was equal to, if not greater than, Stanford's.[34]

As 2012 drew to a close, both platforms were engaged in a pitched battle to win what had become a "surfing the tsunami competition." Koller, Ng, and Agarwal flew around the world, speaking at conferences and universities and meeting with world leaders, all promising to harness technology to democratize education globally. Who could say no? How could one possibly object? What university leader would advocate for sitting on the sidelines when the tsunami was coming?

In April 2013, Stanford joined with edX to create the Open edX Initiative—an offering of open-source code that would enable any institution to host their own MOOCs. As part of the contract terms, Stanford would reassign the engineers and staff who were working on Class2Go to Open edX. And Stanford would send the Class2Go code—the original Coursera source code—to edX.[35] Was this a gift from John Hennessy to one his former PhD students, the CEO of edX, Anant Agarwal? A signal to Koller and Ng that Stanford was hedging its MOOC bet on their biggest rival? A diversion for the higher-education community to obscure Stanford's initial investment of social capital in a for-profit company? Or all three?

6

Riding the Waves

John Hennessy's tsunami never materialized, but while pundits and university leadership were declaring that MOOCs were just another overhyped educational technology, a sea change was occurring, driven indirectly by technology and directly by students. Not only did enrollments in MOOCs increase, but learners began paying for a certificate that proved they had taken the MOOC and passed it.[1] A demographic study conducted by the University of Pennsylvania showed that the majority of MOOC completers had both a job and a college degree.[2] Universities reacted to this news in two ways: they decried Coursera for failing to live up to its mission and they saw a profit opportunity by charging for their courses. In 2015, the Wharton School decided to pursue potential profits by bundling four introductory MOOCs in accounting, corporate finance, marketing, and operations and offering them as a certificate in "Business Foundations."[3] Although initial reception was tepid, this program alone would soon gross $5 million annually in revenue for several years in a row. Other universities, notably Johns Hopkins, the University of Michigan, Duke, and Stanford, also had top-performing certificates, primarily in business and technical skills.[4]

Condemnation of MOOCs in general, and Coursera in particular, was swift, and self-satisfied. Those skeptics who felt you couldn't trust Stanford, or technology companies, or venture capitalists proclaimed that MOOCs were over, just a few years after they had begun.[5] Perhaps no one repeated these claims more fervently than Coursera's competitors, edX and Udacity. In fact, Udacity claimed, in 2017, that "MOOCs are a failed product, at least for the goals we had set for ourselves. . . . Our mission is to bring relevant education which advances people in careers and socio-economic activities, and MOOCs aren't the way."[6] EdX, on the other hand, was somewhat more subtle. Anant Agarwal began visiting Coursera's partners and promising a true "nonprofit," university-created alternative to the untrustworthy alliance of Stanford tech and venture capital. EdX launched a campaign of "converting" Coursera partners into edX partners. Doing so benefited the universities, because they were not beholden to one platform to distribute their content. But the strategy became a double-edged sword for edX, especially as the Coursera platform became more stable, and the company more professionalized, while edX, who initially had a more stable codebase, began to have trouble maintaining a functional platform.

In early 2016, a group of young "Courserians" came to Wharton to present surprising news (I hosted this meeting in my role at Wharton). In the course of research on the demographics of their learners, they found clusters of hundreds if not thousands of people logging into courses from the same location. Further investigation revealed that these locations were huge tech corporations, including Cisco and Amazon. Apparently, those male, college-educated users identified in UPenn's study were logging onto MOOCs to help them advance at work, and they were happy to pay for the experience. This development helped explain why successful certificate programs were in work-relevant topics, for example, Excel skills, accounting, Python, and data science. It also showed that learners, however well educated, were finding certain kinds of MOOCs valuable enough to pay for them.[7]

In the popular imagination, however, MOOCs had failed.[8] They were not replacing universities, solving educational inequities, and lifting legions of underserved learners out of poverty as had been breathlessly foretold in 2012. The fact that they were providing a useful service that people were willing to pay for received little public attention. Many universities dismissed Coursera entirely at this point as being "all about the money" and embraced edX's sales pitch that it was the true nonprofit MOOC provider—even as edX also lobbied universities to attract courses in business and other marketable topics and began charging for them.[9] And while Coursera was beginning to see the glimmerings of a path to profitability, they soon made a misstep.

In 2014, Andrew Ng stepped back from day-to-day operations and Rick Levin, former president of Yale, noted economist and former director of American Express and the Hewlett Foundation, became Coursera's CEO.[10] Levin was hired as what venture capitalists call "the adult in the room": an experienced businessman who shepherds the founders through the scaling and operational phases of the business. Koller and Ng had managed to both create the wave of hype around MOOCs and ride it for two years while growing enrollments exponentially. Now, the company funders felt it was time to corral the company's energy and momentum and steer it toward a business model that would enable Coursera to go public.

Levin's arrival was met initially by university partners with relief and goodwill. Rick was the ultimate insider in higher ed, with a stellar scholarly reputation, sterling administrative credentials, a friendly manner, and a deep appreciation for online learning. His previous involvement in All Learn while president of Yale may have come to nothing except a debit on Yale's balance sheet, but Levin had had many successes in higher ed innovation since.[11] He appreciated Coursera's mission, was highly respected in academia, and understood how the business of higher ed worked.[12] But ultimately, he underestimated the rancor universities felt toward Coursera.

The backlash against Coursera had been a constant high-pitched whine, like a mosquito circling your head, since the company's earliest days.[13] Initial partners were upset with the "bugginess" of the early platform, the frenetic speed with which the company moved, and the highly public nature of the first MOOCs, which universities felt exposed them to brand damage. Although their brands were actually amplified,[14] the platform was fixed, and Coursera was moving at typical start-up speed, the idea that the company was unreliable had taken hold among faculty and staff at a number of institutions across the globe. Publicly, the notion that only 5 percent of learners ever completed a course was seen as a failure, along with the finding that the majority of MOOC completers already held degrees.[15] Universities also cited lack of course completion as a reason to move away from MOOCs, despite multiple studies and data that showed completion rates among learners who paid for courses (or received financial aid) were roughly equal to the number of college students who complete a degree in six years (currently 60 percent).[16] EdX capitalized on these fears, promising more attention to the faculty requests for platform enhancements and a greater focus on student engagement.

Coursera pushed forward, and at its 2016 conference at the Hague, Koller and Levin made two stunning announcements. Coursera was pursuing two new lines of business: online degrees and "business to business" (b2b): selling its content library directly into corporations. Reaction from universities was mixed. While many assumed Coursera would move into online degrees, they were primarily concerned with the first offering's cost—a mere $22,000 for an MBA from the University of Illinois, a highly ranked public university.[17] Given that students at top 10 business schools pay nearly ten times as much for the same degree, business schools in the mid-range of the rankings, whose tuition for a two-year degree is in the six figures, wondered how they could retain students in the face of this new, lower-priced offering. But it was the other initiative, selling existing MOOCs to corporations who would then give access to their employees, that created a fault line in the relationship between Coursera and some of its prestige partner universities.

When Coursera decided to begin selling MOOCs directly to businesses for corporate training or professional development, Levin and Koller positioned it as a way to "upskill" workers and provide economic opportunity across the globe.[18] Universities agreed with this noble mission; however, they disagreed with the new pricing model Coursera was offering them for b2b sales. Coursera had always operated on a revenue share basis with university partners: of every dollar a learner paid to Coursera, a certain percentage went to the university (and percentages varied by university).[19] As part of this relationship, the university had control over branding, advertising, and pricing of its courses. But the new "Coursera for business" revenue share model gave Coursera almost total control over the price of the courses and also cut the university partner's revenue share by as much as 25 percent. A number of universities found this development mildly concerning, but a group of name-brand universities, including Stanford, the University of Pennsylvania, and the University of Michigan, were highly upset. Losing control of pricing meant that Coursera would be able to sell university content for a fraction of what the set price was and, perhaps more importantly, would sell courses as a bundle, with no clear differentiation between universities. For the Wharton School, this was unacceptable. Wharton MOOCs were always supposed to be priced slightly higher than any other MOOC on the platform in order to signal that the content was of higher value. School leadership felt that bundling Wharton content into a corporate sale would be akin to selling someone a grab bag of clothing, with a few designer (Wharton) pieces included. This bundling at a cheap price was perceived as a direct threat not just to Wharton's brand but also to Wharton's executive education arm, which was selling online courses to corporations through its Wharton Online brand (in the interest of full disclosure, I established and led Wharton Online through its first five years). Stanford, the University of Michigan, and others also protested this loss of control. Koller left the company in late summer of 2016,[20] and Levin began a protracted, yearlong set of negotiations with multiple dissenting university partners, flying all over the country for meetings with provosts, deans, vice provosts, vice deans, and associate deans to plead his case. In the end, almost every university capitulated and agreed to have Coursera sell their MOOC content into corporations. However, Levin's time at Coursera was coming to a close, and Coursera's board began to search for a new leader.[21] And meanwhile, the practice of fractionalizing university courses for increased profit continued.

The Great Unbundling

Indeed, the ways that digital technology is talked about within educational circles certainly extenuate superficial, ephemeral and often banal aspects of the topic at the expense of any sustained engagement with its messy politics.... Similarly, this is language that offers scant insight into the political economy of an education technology marketplace reckoned to be worth in excess of $5 trillion. When seen from any of these perspectives, then education and technology can be justifiably criticized as a site of organized forgetting.[22]

—NEAL SELWYN

Anant Agarwal, president and CEO of edX, bounded across the stage at the Fairmont Hotel in Georgetown Washington, DC. It was November 2015. Standing before a crowd of a hundred or so university provosts, deans, and senior administrators from the most elite universities in the United States, he proudly introduced MicroMasters, a process by which a learner could exchange a series of certificates of completion from free MOOCs into a year's worth of credits toward a master's degree. Agarwal introduced two metaphors to explain how the process worked, both of which "decomposed" traditional university degree processes. (In computer science, "decomposition" describes the process of breaking a large problem into smaller, more manageable sub-problems.)[23]

First, Agarwal used the term "unbundling" to mean disaggregating an educational experience into separate parts such as course content, course delivery, and course credential to explain how higher education was being broken apart by new technologies. Second, he used the term "stacking" to refer to how these unbundled components would be able to fit together in new ways that would be beneficial to the learner—giving them more control over when and where they learned and, to some extent, what they learned. Although both "unbundling" and "stacking" could be seen as a dire threat to the traditional model of higher education, both could also provide economies of scale and new sources of revenue.[24] For instance, by using free MOOCs as a way to replace the first year of a two-year master's degree, MIT would be able to decrease their advertising dollars and admissions resources while doubling enrollment in the program.

Agarwal defined the "unbundled" pieces as the clock, the content, and the credential. "The clock" represented the time learners spent to earn a degree. "The content" was the lectures, assignments, and ideas of the teacher captured by technology and delivered at the student's convenience. "The credential" used to refer solely to a degree but could now be anything: a MOOC statement of completion, work experience, course credit. Some of these units, like content delivery and assessment, could be scaled massively through online delivery. Some units could be delivered on campus. All would be marked by certification upon completion. And each was "unbundled" by the technological capabilities and learner behavior that arose from 2011 to 2015 during the early years of MOOCs. The audience was abuzz for the rest of the conference, thinking we were witnessing something brand-new from one of the most innovative institutions of higher education in the world.

At the coffee break, I spoke with Vince Price, then provost of the University of Pennsylvania (as of this writing, president of Duke University), about how UPenn could engage in more innovation in online education. We compared the cultures and appetites for seemingly disruptive practices at both UPenn and Stanford, and our excitement about the coming disruption of higher education was tinged with no small amount of trepidation.[25] We needn't have worried. What no one at the conference said, or mostly likely knew, was that the new technologies and practices we were experimenting with to "scale" high-quality education for working adults and underserved communities not only were quite similar to the highly successful practices of profit-making used by private equity–backed for-profit institutions over the previous fifteen years[26] but were also using "new" technologies that had been envisioned a half century before that.

Five months later, Agarwal gave the same presentation to a similar audience at Stanford as part of a panel titled "The Future of Academic Credentials."[27] The fellow panelists were Lou Pugliese, former CEO of Blackboard and current Senior Innovation Fellow at Arizona State University; Carolyn Levander, vice president of Digital Education at Rice University; Jake Schwartz, cofounder of General Assembly, a software bootcamp; and myself, representing Wharton Online. Each of our organizations certified learners for coursework that did not bear traditional credits toward a degree but might under a new system of unbundling and stacking. In the few short months since the edX conference in DC, noncredit certificates from both traditional and nontraditional education providers were exploding in number.[28] I presented on our nascent success with Wharton Online, showing seventy-five thousand certificates earned in just the previous year. "We are printing a currency that we do not back," I said of Wharton/UPenn. "We are asking the learners to create value by exchanging this MOOC certificate for a better job or for course credit. The credential itself is totally made up." My belief in the innovation of this model was soon shaken by one of the conference program chairs, Stanford sociologist Mitchell Stevens, who added, "It's the same as degrees, Anne.... They're all made up." Stevens was one of the few academics who participated in the discussions about MOOCs and higher education disruption who also had not developed amnesia about the practices of higher education itself. Agarwal, Koller, and Ng arguably felt pressure from their investors to sell something new that would "democratize" education, but few others questioned why education, particularly public education, needed to be democratized at all.

In fact, while edX's MicroMasters were seen as a new product for elite universities, many community colleges and state universities had been offering "stackable" credentials for decades. What was unique to MicroMasters was the cost savings: completing a MicroMasters and then matriculating at a university and earning the associated degree saved the learner about 40 percent of the tuition of a two-year master's degree program, while the university was able to double enrollment and reduce marketing costs. MIT was the first university to offer a MicroMaster (in supply chain management) and others followed suit, including Georgia Tech, the University of Pennsylvania, the University of Michigan, the University of Maryland Global Campus, and several global universities. At the same time, edX launched an initiative in partnership with Arizona State University that enabled learners to receive college credit for MOOCs. Initially called Global Freshman Academy, the program pioneered the "pay if you pass" model for learners (ultimately, not enough learners passed and the initiative was repurposed).[29] EdX was also selling courses into companies, but they were doing so in a manner that had greater appeal to universities: the university had more latitude in setting the price for the learner, as well as greater visibility into which corporations were using the courses.[30]

As these innovations and disruptions continued, a number of universities decided they did not want to partner with either edX or Coursera, and they also wanted to sell courses online. Most quickly realized that building a functional platform is hard work (edX's struggles with providing a stable platform that was not subject to litigation served as a warning for many).[31] What if there was a way for a university to outsource the marketing and delivery of online courses to a vendor, while still maintaining brand and price control? Most universities didn't want to conquer the world; they just wanted to capture learners who could not come to campus for a residential degree. A number of companies, called Online Program Managers (OPMs), were prepared to do just that.

The Golden Loophole

Since 1992, universities have been prohibited from spending federal funds (including student loans) on incentivized enrollment programs offered by OPMs. This policy was designed to keep OPMs from rewarding salespeople, or "enrollment counselors" (as they are known), for being paid per student enrollment, which resulted in unsuspecting learners, particularly minorities and veterans, taking out student loans to sign up for college programs that were essentially worthless (if they completed them), saddling the learner with student loan debt they would be unlikely to ever have the means to repay. But in 2011, 2U's CEO, Chip Paucek, among others, successfully lobbied the Education Department to issue an amendment to this policy. The amendment enabled universities to share tuition dollars (including those that came from student loans) with OPMs for recruiting, as long as other activities such as student support, technology, and marketing were included in the "bundled services" that the OPM provided. Because OPMs could now aggressively market to and recruit students using the student's own loans, universities and OPMs would make more money the way any other business does—through price optimization. In other words, the OPMs and universities would maximize profit by finding the maximum number of students at the maximum price for the product. Initially, at universities such as the University of North Carolina, the University of Southern California (USC), and Berkeley, the maximum price was the same as, if not slightly more than, the in-person experience. The maximum number of students, however, was many times more than these universities could teach in person, making OPM-supported online degree programs a valuable source of revenue for the university and justifying the high marketing costs. Universities then used inflated customer acquisition costs as justification for keeping tuition high, despite the economies of scale realized through offering the courses online. And because some OPMs charged as much as 94 percent of total revenue for each student they enrolled in the programs, universities trapped in these arrangements could honestly claim that they weren't bringing in enormous amounts of revenue per program, as a significant portion of the student's tuition money was being funneled to the OPM.[32]

"Let's Wash This Money through the Laundromat"

—NAS, "AFFIRMATIVE ACTION"

Today, investors in OPMs get rich the same way that private equity investors in for-profit colleges do: by converting federal student loan dollars into private wealth. 2U's founder, John

Katzman, who left the company in 2012, "likes to joke that the acronym also stands for 'other people's money.'"[33] What Katzman doesn't say is that those "other people" are working adults, single parents, veterans, and minority learners.[34] Imagine a learner who enrolls in USC's online master's degree in social work operated by 2U. Assuming you are part of the 69 percent of USC students who pass the national licensing exam after your program, your average salary two years after graduation would be $52,000 a year, leaving you with an approximately $300 monthly student debt payment just for your tuition and fees.[35] 2U, which has pocketed anywhere from nearly $70,000 of your money, spends it on employee salaries, digital advertising (Google, Facebook, LinkedIn), and executive salaries. As a publicly traded company whose market capitalization whipsawed between $5.5 billion (June 2018) and $103 million (November 2023),[36] 2U was a target for both investors and private equity takeover. The company eventually declared bankruptcy in the summer of 2024 and reemerged as a privately held company, saddling stockholders with $500 million in losses.[37]

But the shadow OPMs cast on providing value for a learner goes seemingly unnoticed by universities that continue to partner with them, some at their own peril. A 2022 report on OPMs by the Government Accountability Office (GAO) noted that 550 U.S. universities had a partnership with an OPM. These partnership contracts are difficult to access and often protected by NDAs or clauses asking public universities to refer Freedom of Information Act requests to the OPM instead of the universities' own legal counsel. And universities are generally not in the business of sharing contracts with each other. Together, these conditions combine to form a haze of secrecy around OPM tuition sharing, length of contract, and services provided. Instead, universities scour each other's websites and have unofficial conversations with their colleagues at other universities to try to seek clarity on the "best practices" of OPMs—and partnering with them.[38]

For the most part, the larger, wealthier universities can weather whatever storms may come from an OPM partnership. Even in the case of USC, whose partnership with 2U was the subject of unflattering press,[39] undergraduate applications remained robust, with 71,000 applications for undergraduate admissions for the fall of 2021. These application numbers are even more remarkable considering that shortly before the revelations about 2U, USC had been revealed as a major player in the Varsity Blues college admissions scandal,[40] and the year before that, the university was accused of turning a blind eye to the off-campus exploits of the medical school dean, who raised $1 billion for the university while smoking meth in hotel rooms with young prostitutes, one of whom died while with him.[41] The fact that a few thousand online master's degree students did not get the educational experience they were promised or paid for seems to pale in comparison. And even though USC's online programs through 2U struggled since the revelations, the university is well positioned to financially weather the financial storm the troubled partnership produces given its $8.1 billion endowment.[42] In fact, USC was able to wind down its agreement with 2U in 2023 and host its online programs itself.

For universities with smaller endowments and student populations, however, partnership with an OPM can eat away at the school's residential programs and ultimately cause a loss of overall revenue as well as control of the institution itself. Erik Gilbert, a professor of history at Arkansas State University, described the consequences of the university's decade-plus-long contract with Academic Partnerships, a well-known OPM that is now owned by a private equity firm, Vistria, which also owns the Apollo Education group, the largest for-profit education provider in the United States. Arkansas State offered one of Academic Partnerships' first degree programs, a master's in education (M.Ed.). This program resulted in a 10 percent increase in the institution's overall enrollment, which was seen as a great success. Ten years later, while enrollments have held steady, the university's financial position has declined because of its dealings with Academic Partnerships. As of 2021, 40 percent of Arkansas State's student body was enrolled by Academic Partnerships, leaving classrooms empty, cafeterias and parking lots deserted, and dorm rooms gathering dust. Online students may be cheaper to educate because they do not take up as much faculty time, but they also don't spend money on food, shelter, and socializing on and around campus. Gilbert sums up the situation as follows: "That's a big deal at mid-tier institutions like mine, where fees are a big source of revenue. Here at ASU, the rule of thumb is that it takes three students in an OPM-run program to create the same revenue as one on-campus student. . . . As a result, despite a nominally stable enrollment, we have been lurching from one budget crisis to another."[43] A report from the Century Foundation found this was not uncommon among smaller public universities that have contracts with Academic Partnerships. Southeastern Oklahoma University also sees 40 percent of its students enrolled and managed by Academic Partnerships; Lamar University, part of the Texas State University system, has 50 percent of its students serviced by Academic Partnerships. Based on enrollments, each of these universities should be doing well, but given the volume of learners and tuition dollars being shared with the private equity–backed OPM, they are being slowly starved.[44]

Although degree students are high-value targets for OPMs, they are more expensive to acquire and support than noncredit learners—those who want a certificate in computer or business skills. Noncredit certificate learners also don't use federal student loans to pay for their course fees, and so the potential for federal regulation or oversight is almost nonexistent. And while each noncredit enrollment brings in far fewer dollars than a degree enrollment, these certificates can be much more lucrative for both the universities and the OPMs, since there is no guarantee that the course will feature any student-faculty interaction with professors at the sponsoring institution. In addition, the revenue share arrangements for these programs can tilt in favor of the OPM, since they are often also recruiting instructors and providing the virtual classroom technology for the students.

For example, the University of Pennsylvania School of Liberal and Professional Studies struck a deal with Trilogy bootcamps (owned by 2U) and, in 2022, offered three coding bootcamps in data science, cybersecurity, and coding. The tuition for each is $13,000.[45] According to the industry average, Penn would receive $2,600 for each student, primarily for allowing Trilogy/2U to use Penn's website and to use Penn's logo on the certificate of completion. The remaining $10,400 is retained by 2U/Trilogy for providing instruction. Students, however, assume they are receiving instruction from Penn, or any other university that partners with 2U/Trilogy to host these bootcamps. This is a deliberate effort on the part of both the university and the OPM, as students will pay a higher premium for a Penn certificate than a Trilogy certificate. And the reason students will pay a brand premium for a noncredit certificate of completion is the reasonable belief that employers and others value a certificate from Penn more than Trilogy.

Nowhere is this more true, perhaps, than the $50,000 noncredit certificate in business analytics from Harvard.[46] To earn the certificate, students take six asynchronous (prerecorded) courses, participate in two virtual seminars, and come to campus for two long weekends. In return they receive a certificate from Harvard. While the virtual sessions are taught by Harvard faculty, and the in-person campus visits include a few case study sessions with faculty, the bulk of the instructional material is delivered by 2U. Because of the higher involvement of Harvard faculty, I was told that Harvard retained at least 40 percent of the revenue per student. This noncredit certificate was a huge success, with upwards of 600 students enrolled per year. That translates to $30 million in revenue a year, with roughly $12 million going to Harvard and the other $18 million going to 2U. By comparison, an MBA at Harvard costs approximately $150,000 in tuition, or $75,000 per year at list price, which most students don't pay due to generous scholarship packages. In 2022, tuition dollars made up almost 14 percent of Harvard Business School's income, while noncredit certificates, both online and in-person, represented nearly twice as much with a combined 26 percent of revenue.[47]

Clearly noncredit education pays, at least when it comes from a name-brand school. 2U made the strategic acquisition of the South African MOOC provider GetSmarter in 2017 (for $103 million) and Trilogy in 2019 (for $750 million) to expand its capabilities in offering noncredit certificates and provide a hedge against federal oversight of their online degree programs.[48] In fact, the market for noncredit certificates, which includes professional development, executive education, and "upskilling" (training in new technologies), is estimated to be half a trillion dollars by 2025.[49] This new market is unproven, unregulated, and up for grabs. The oft-dismissed $40 MOOC certificates from Coursera in 2015 opened a profit opportunity to universities that a rogue's gallery of OPMs and edtech companies began racing to fill.

Is This What We Meant by Globalization?

"India to Become the EdTech Capital of the World"
—HEADLINE FROM THE INDIA BRAND EQUITY FOUNDATION, A GOVERNMENT WEBSITE

Early enrollments in both Coursera and edX MOOCs revealed a tremendous appetite for free online courses in what are known as the BRIC countries: Brazil, Russia, India, and China. India in particular sparked the interest of universities and venture capital, as it represented an enormous market for U.S. education. A 2019 KPMG report concluded that India was the second largest market for "e-learning" after the United States, and the online education market in India is expected to grow by US $2.28 billion during 2021–25.[50] For U.S. universities, MOOC platforms became an easy way to access the Indian market, which had been off-limits, given the complexities of collecting revenue and delivering education in the region.

Indian entrepreneurs and investors were looking at this same data and reacted by creating a series of edtech platforms and OPMs that delivered U.S. content. Companies such as UpGrad, Emeritus, Simplilearn, and Great Learning expanded from offering U.S. university courses to the Indian market to offering U.S. university courses to the U.S. market, often by "recycling" existing MOOC content and wrapping it in a set of services that include marketing, enrollment, tutoring, and student support. They are nearly indistinguishable from the top U.S. OPMs except they can provide enrollment and student support at much lower prices, since they primarily use employees in India to provide these services. For example, Emeritus began offering a noncredit online certificate from the Wharton School in business analytics in 2018 for $2,750. The course consisted of a set of videos curated from the Wharton Online Business Analytics Specialization on Coursera, available for free or approximately $400 for a certificate (financial aid is also available). The version on Coursera consists of four courses and a capstone project, or approximately twenty weeks of instruction. The Emeritus business analytics program is hosted in Canvas, a popular learning management system, and is twelve weeks long. Unlike the Coursera program, business analytics from Emeritus features Zoom sessions with a professor and teaching assistants hired by Emeritus. The experience is higher touch; yet the most marked difference between the two programs is the certificate, which for the Emeritus course is nearly indistinguishable from a Wharton executive education certificate.

Emeritus supercharged its partnerships with the Wharton business analytics certificate. Although the company had been acting as an OPM for a few programs for Columbia and MIT, as well as a lone course from Harvard Business School (the founder, Ashwin Demara, was an HBS alum), it faced difficulty attracting new partners because of both its relatively small size and its reputation for aggressive marketing practices that elite universities found unseemly. Demara realized he needed to provide a value proposition to elite universities that they could not refuse, so he devised a solution that would activate the universities' "buy as a pack" mentality as well as their desire for revenue: he would add Wharton as a partner and ensure the school was profitable. In order to do so, all he had to do was offer guaranteed revenue to the school.

Demara's approach was successful. Wharton's business analytics revenue exceeded the guaranteed minimums, and he began combing the Wharton Online course catalog for other programs to offer; to date, Wharton offers over twenty programs through Emeritus, the majority of which are also offered on Coursera for far less. Peer universities began to sign up, including Berkeley, Northwestern, Dartmouth, London Business School, and Cambridge, in addition to MIT and Columbia. Emeritus's parent company, Eruditus, is a unicorn—a start-up valued at $1 billion or more, reaching a US $3.2 billion valuation in 2021.[51] Other companies like UpGrad and Simplilearn have followed this approach, harvesting existing online content from top schools and offering it with offshore student enrollment and instructional support. The profit potential from these companies has inflated expectations: from a base of US $700–800 million in 2021, the Indian edtech market is projected to reach US $30 billion by 2031.[52] These profits are accruing to U.S. investment firms, as Sequoia India, GSV Ventures, Chan Zuckerberg, Silver Lake Partners, and Leeds, among others, are all providing capital to the Indian edtech market.

OPMs Zig, Coursera Zags

Just as soon as edtech companies were being started and acquired to provide access to the market for noncredit certificates Coursera and edX opened up, Coursera decided to focus on online degrees. Jeff Maggioncalda, an experienced executive, took the CEO role at Coursera in 2017 and immediately began lobbying partner universities to put online master's degrees on the platform. He won a few key partners (University of Pennsylvania, University of Michigan, Arizona State, University of Colorado-Boulder, and Imperial College, London) with a simple argument: Coursera could help expand master's degree programs without high customer-acquisition costs or running afoul of the federal government.[53] It would use its large customer base to market degrees and pass the savings on to the students. Instead of charging $100,000 or more for an online master's degree, Coursera would charge an average of $25,000. Universities would provide instruction, learner support, grading, and the degree, while Coursera would provide enrollments and the platform. Under this arrangement universities would realize profits from scaling the programs, and they could still argue that they were fulfilling their mission of expanding access to education without keeping their fingers crossed behind their back.

Coursera hadn't forgotten about noncredit certificates, however. During this period, they introduced two new types of certificates: MasterTrack and Professional certificates. MasterTrack certificates were a relatively faithful copy of edX's MicroMaster programs—a series of courses that could "stack" into a degree. Professional certificates were offered not by universities but by companies teaching the technical skills they required entry-level employees to learn. Professional certificates, which often featured industry partners that would accept the certificate in lieu of a degree as a job requirement, began to find a larger and larger audience. Today, they are the most popular noncredit certificates offered on Coursera, although many community colleges and some universities accept these courses for college credit.[54]

By early 2020, with the exception of Harvard, MIT, Stanford, Cornell, ASU, and the primarily online universities (Western Governors, Southern New Hampshire), universities had handed over their online degree and certificate programs to a set of OPMs and edtech platforms that were setting prices, instructional standards, and marketing and enrollment practices. The lucky universities were receiving additional revenue and generating valuable brand exposure. The rest weren't as fortunate. Most importantly, the learners who were supposed to be helped by gaining access to higher education were less likely to complete their degrees and more likely to struggle with repaying student loan debt.[55]

Universities are, by definition, filled with very smart people. Yet their response to online education over the past decade has resulted in them being taken advantage of by for-profit companies. What choices did universities make to find themselves operating online programs according to the same playbook used by for-profit colleges? The answers are unique to each institution, but a few common missteps have emerged that even the most wealthy and elite universities have taken.

1. *Not using evidence-based research when selecting educational technology.*
   a. Decision makers in higher ed are more likely to rely on market demand and internal pressure to expand access to higher education in choosing educational technology than evidence-based research on student outcomes. And while many new technologies promise results before scientifically rigorous research is available, universities rarely consider research conducted in another context as they believe their own students and faculty are unique.[56]
2. *Doing what everyone else is doing.*
   a. Universities have a "buy as a pack" mentality that edtech platforms exploit to drive adoption and create market share.
   b. Each university is unique, however, with regard to their revenue share agreements with OPMs, which range from 20 to 94 percent.[57]

3. *Appointing faculty members, or a faculty committee, to make business decisions.*
   a. Tenured faculty are risk averse, competitive, and unionized. Most also don't have significant experience negotiating with billion-dollar companies. OPMs and edtech platforms love to negotiate with faculty because faculty don't have the same interests as students, who are the platform's ultimate customers.
   b. Tenured faculty are sheltered from the financial consequences of their actions, unlike their students, who may spend a lifetime paying off the debt they incurred to be taught by these same faculty.
4. *Not recognizing the homogeneity of innovation experts.*
   a. Homogeneity of experts leads to homogeneity of strategy, which universities generally like because the strategy appears less risky. Consider that an influential number of online learning strategists at universities share the following characteristics with venture capitalists and edtech platform CEOs: they are male, have an MBA or PhD from a top 10 school, know all the same people, and are deeply passionate about reforming education.[58] They convene several times a year at ASU-GSV, South by Southwest, and invite-only conferences. Many of these people are my friends and I know them to be smart and genuinely interested in improving education. But how can any of us be creating a future of higher education that includes more opportunities for underserved learners when we have very little idea what that means? More importantly, why aren't we wondering why venture capital and private equity are suddenly concerned

with the educational struggles of minorities, working adults, and veterans?
5. *Ignoring that venture capitalists do more than fund edtech.*
   a. Universities underestimate the extent to which venture capitalists determine the narrative around the mission of the university and the need for edtech to fulfill that mission. Investors in edtech firms claim their platforms "extend access" and "democratize education" without acknowledging that these phrases legitimize massive growth as a force for social impact while ignoring that scaling successfully (e.g., Coursera and edX) can bring enormous profits to the investors.[59]

An underlying factor in each of these missteps is embedded in the hierarchy of the university: where faculty are privileged above staff, no matter how senior or expert in their fields. The two-class system at universities is exploited by OPMs and platforms; if a staff member recommends actions in contradiction with the OPM's best interests, then the OPM will go to a faculty member to plead their case, knowing full well that the desires and opinions of the faculty member will almost always prevail over the recommendation of staff.[60] Both large OPMs and small edtech companies deploy this strategy in order to get universities to sign them on as vendors. The staff who sometimes do break through (see "innovation experts" above) are closer to the interests of venture capital than learners, whether they recognize it or not. Universities will not have equitable and effective online learning strategies until the underserved learners and qualified staff have a voice in the discussion that is equal to that of faculty.

By late 2019 and early 2020, more master's degrees were being offered online than ever before,[61] and those accessed through Coursera and edX were inexpensive, at scale, and from name-brand institutions. Coursera was advancing relentlessly toward its goal of going public. EdX, whose comparatively lackluster enrollments, buggy platform, and lack of profits began to turn off university partners, was gamely launching degree programs. It appeared that higher education had dismissed online learning as an existential threat and was looking toward its next crisis—artificial intelligence and the future of work. In 2018, the World Economic Forum released its first "Future of Jobs" report,[62] which was quickly followed by McKinsey's research on automation and the workforce, both with a similar message: hundreds of millions of jobs were at risk of being changed or eliminated because of AI and automation, leading to a crisis in education.[63] How should universities respond? How would they ensure that their courses were relevant in an age of AI? Could AI ever replace teaching?

The fear of AI displacing teachers was overstated. In 2019, AI for education was not a growth area for investment compared with security, robotic process automation (RPA), data management, and health care. (The largest Series A in the United States in 2018 [$550 million] was awarded to Automation Anywhere, which provides RPA processes for back-office accounting and other tasks.)[64] Even though a number of AI processes touch higher education, the market opportunity for using AI directly to scale, distribute, or enhance education remains smaller than in other sectors.

In 2019 most universities were using AI "secondhand" in marketing, cybersecurity, or student-support technologies. Many developed courses and programs of study in AI or related topics; however, these efforts suffered from the mismatch between the rapid pace of technological advancement and the time required to create and teach a course. In response, software companies began to provide their own training to corporations, universities, and learners (Automation Anywhere, IBM, Google) using platforms like Coursera and edX, potentially cutting out the "middleman" of the university. Capitalizing on this development, in China and Africa, "learning centers" that provide human coaching and asynchronous education were opened as an alternative to higher education. In this model, learners pay a membership fee to a center that provides up-to-date online training from technology companies throughout the learner's lifespan, bypassing the university entirely.[65] In theory, those who participate in learning centers will have more in-demand knowledge and job-relevant skills than a traditional college graduate.

The surge of online courses supplied the raw material of AI: vast quantities of learner data. Some universities established learning analytics centers to support research into the "measurement, collection, analysis and reporting of data about learners and their contexts, for purposes of understanding and optimizing learning and the environments in which it occurs."[66] This field is the truest expression of Pat Suppes's and Don Bitzer's work, as it is both academic and commercial: much of the data on learner behavior is collected in technological learning environments, and the findings about learning are meant to inform the design and delivery of education in these environments. Learning analytics uses data science, machine learning, and AI to create the best use of technology to enhance learning. As Ryan Baker, head of UPenn's Learning Analytics Center, wrote, "To sum up, the ultimate goal of the field of Artificial Intelligence in Education is not to promote artificial intelligence, but to promote education. . . . In the end, our goal is not to create intelligent tutoring systems or stupid tutoring systems, but to create intelligent and successful students."[67] Scholars seemed to have a handle on AI in education, and the threat appeared to have been averted.

Then in March 2020, the world shut down. But everyone's computer stayed on.

7

Covid, Cash-Outs, and ChatGPT

> Edtech start-ups raised record amounts of venture capital in 2020 and 2021, and market valuations for bigger players soared.
>
> —MCKINSEY, *HOW TECHNOLOGY IS SHAPING LEARNING HIGHER EDUCATION*, 2022

Higher education was forced to shift nearly all classes online in March 2020, and many institutions continued to operate virtually for the next eighteen months. As millions of students began attending "Zoom U," they called the value proposition of residential higher education into question. A number of universities, including Penn State, Georgetown, American University, and Harvard, were sued by their students for failing to provide in-person education. Although these lawsuits were largely unsuccessful, they did reflect the expectations of students and families "that the bargain between universities, students and their families in exchange for tens of thousands of tuition and fee charges each semester is more than just a bargain for credits and nothing more."[1] And although some institutions, including Princeton, reduced tuition nominally (10 percent) and/or did not charge activities or athletics fees,[2] others continued to charge the full complement of tuition and fees for offering classes 100 percent remotely—refusing to unbundle prices even as the pandemic constrained their services primarily to teaching, assessment, and certification.

At the same time, enrollments in MOOCs at both Coursera and edX soared—nearly doubling to 70 million for Coursera and topping out at 39 million at edX. These massive enrollment increases were driven, in part, by promotions offered by the platforms. For instance, Coursera offered its catalog free of charge to universities and governments around the world, driving new customer growth.[3] These promotions, spearheaded by American universities such as Duke, were presented to the public as a humanitarian effort, connecting learners around the globe to education for free. "We are just a facilitator," said Coursera's CEO, Jeff Maggioncalda, in his 2020 Coursera conference keynote.[4] This statement was not untrue, but it also wasn't the whole story. Coursera and edX would use the stunning increase in users to position themselves for future profit: Coursera would file for an IPO less than a year later, and edX would be acquired shortly after that. Perhaps both companies were inspired by Winston Churchill, who is credited with saying, "Never let a good crisis go to waste."[5]

The increased interest in MOOCs concealed a more troubling statistic, however. College enrollment declined during the pandemic.[6] A variety of factors, including demographic trends, an increasing number of learners who "stopped out" of college without earning a degree, and declining belief in the value of higher education combined to create a smaller pool of first-time college enrollments.[7] In response, universities are seeking to

The Wonderful World of Credentials

Type	Definition	Example	Quality control
Badge	Electronic symbol shared on social media	Wharton Online Alumni	Set by issuer
MOOC certificate	Pdf, Social media badge	Multiple Coursera, edX courses	Assessments
Specialization certificate	Pdf, Social media badge	Multiple Coursera specializations	Passing grouped courses
Noncredit certificate	Pdf/paper certificate	Individual EE programs, groups of EE programs	Attendance, payment
Credit-eligible certificate	Paper certificate with transcript credit	MicroMasters, et al.	**Admissions**, assessments, set curriculum
Credit-bearing certificate	Paper certificate with transcript credit	Individual schools within university	**Admissions**, assessments, set curriculum
Degree	Paper certificate with transcript credit	BA, MA, MBA, MD, JD, PhD, etc.	**Admissions**, assessments, set curriculum

Definitions

- **Digital badges:** An electronic badge or symbol used to signify skills acquisition or other achievements.
- **MOOC certificate:** Upon successfully completing a MOOC, learners receive a digital certificate that they can display on social media or print out.
- **Digital credentials and microcredentials:** These refer to both badges and digital certificates and encompass any credential smaller than a degree.
- **Certificate:** Paper/pdf recognition of successful completion of a program of study. Can represent courses for-credit courses that are credit-eligible, or noncredit courses. Certificates have swelled to become the second most common postsecondary award in the United States: over 1 million are awarded each year.

FIGURE 9. Different types of education credentials.

develop revenue streams outside of tuition. One market segment being pursued by universities is adults with some college credits but no degree. These learners could be enticed to return to higher education through schools of continuing education as part-time students, earning credit-bearing certificates that would be relevant to their profession and "stack" to a degree. The other market segment is noncredit certificates, much like what Coursera and edX sell but at higher prices and with more support and incentives. This market is highly analogous to executive education programs offered by brand-name institutions, most of whom incentivize learners with the prospect of alumni status for attending a program that costs between fifty and ninety thousand dollars (Harvard Business School offers four of these programs).[8] Currently, a student seeking online education that is not a degree program must navigate a confusing mix of programs with different credentials. These prospective students are left on their own to determine whether or not the certificate is eligible for university credit, whether it is valued by employers, and even whether or not university staff are involved in teaching and assessing a program, as some programs outsource even that core function, despite offering a certificate for completion with the university name.[9]

After Covid, more universities reached out to OPMs to offer online programs that would help generate revenue from new sets of learners. Yet, with the addition of each new online degree or certificate, advertising to attract learners became more and more expensive. As enrollments in free courses were climbing, the cost of getting learners to pay for courses kept rising. Customer acquisition costs (CAC) reached record highs. For education start-ups like Coursera, Emeritus, and edX, spending for customers was funded by venture capital. But for universities, the funds to acquire customers (through OPMs like 2U, Wiley, Academic Partnerships, and Pearson) had to be paid for with school revenue, which was usually comprised, at least in part, of tuition dollars, a portion of which was federal money in the form of student loans.[10]

This transfer of federal student loan dollars to Google and Facebook through advertising spending did not go unnoticed by the federal government. Just before the pandemic, in January 2020, Senators Elizabeth Warren and Sherrod Brown sent letters to the CEOs of 2U, Academic Partnerships, Bisk Education, Pearson Learning, and Wiley Education Services, requesting copies of the contracts OPMs had with universities, as well as marketing and other materials. "It is also critical that policymakers determine if OPM business practices—specifically OPM contracts that require tuition-sharing arrangements—are legal, an appropriate use of federal student aid dollars, and in the best interest of students," the senators wrote.[11]

2U, Wiley, and Pearson provided some financial data to the senators, even as they moved away from revenue sharing as a business model, opting instead to require institutions to pay a "fee for service." In this scenario, the university acts as a sort of money launderer for the OPM, turning federal student loan dollars into payments for advertising. But because the OPM is not sharing in tuition revenue, the OPM can escape government scrutiny and potential oversight. And even though the 2020 letter did not cause an immediate decline in 2U's stock price, the company took a relatively radical step in 2021 to both cut customer acquisition costs and avoid federal scrutiny. They purchased edX for $800 million.[12]

Cashing In and Out

EdX Is Acquired

In June 2021, edX, the avowedly not-for-profit, Harvard and MIT MOOC platform that continually positioned itself as "of the university, by the university for the university" in contrast to the for-profit Stanford platform, Coursera, sold itself to the largest for-profit OPM, 2U, for nearly $1 billion. 2U explained the strategic rationale for the acquisition as having six core benefits: leveraging edX's brand equity, building a scalable marketing advantage, expanding offerings to create a "free to degree" set of programs, growing 2U's global footprint, growing enterprise revenue, and using the highly scalable platform technology. A "key takeaway" for investors was that the addition of edX's 39 million registered learners to 2U's marketing database was expected to generate annual marketing cost efficiencies of 10–15 percent, or $40–60 million per year. While this transaction seemed like a good deal for 2U, it was a great deal for Harvard and MIT, who pocketed $800 million on an $80 million investment that had yet to turn a profit. (On a nonprofit reporting basis, FYE June 30, 2020, edX generated revenue of $84.7 million and operating loss of $17.4 million.) As edtech journalist Michael Feldstein wrote, "When 2U swooped in, that gave MIT and Harvard an opportunity to get out of that money trap, declare victory, and make a handsome return on their investment."[13]

And what would Harvard and MIT plan to do with their nearly billion-dollar windfall? The edX press release announcing the deal claimed that "proceeds of the transaction will go to a nonprofit led by Harvard and MIT focused on transforming educational outcomes, tackling learning inequities."[14] The sale was completed in the fall of 2021, with the full revenue due to be recognized by Harvard and MIT in 2025. Plans for the nonprofit have yet to be revealed, but this lack of transparency has not been questioned by edX's other 160 university partners. *Harvard Magazine* noted, "Few details about the nonprofit's organization or means of operation appear to have been worked out, and fewer still have been disclosed; it will apparently have a joint governing board consisting of four representatives each from Harvard and MIT: for now, the same people who serve on edX's board."[15]

Alongside the blind faith in the ability of Harvard and MIT to steward the transformation of education and resolve the inequalities on which they have built their business models, 2U's

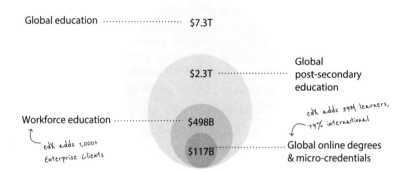

FIGURE 10. From 2U's investor's deck on the purchase of edX. 2U, "Press Release Financials," *Transforming Digital Education*, June 29, 2021, https://www.prnewswire.com/news-releases/2u-inc-and-edx-to-join-together-in-industry-redefining-combination-301321747.html.

acquisition of edX also publicly revealed the enormous market for online and digital education, particularly in the "lifelong learning" category, consisting of noncredit certificates and badges, online degrees, and workforce education. While venture capitalists investing in edtech had long been aware of the profit potential for lifelong learning, many more universities realized exactly how much money they could make by using technology to widen the distribution channels for their programs, and they began offering programs to this new market in an attempt to attract revenue, some of which came from federal student loans.

While federal oversight applies to programs that are eligible for student loans, not all online programs accept them. The majority of noncredit certificates (i.e., microcredentials and workforce development) are not eligible for financial aid; as such, the field is totally unregulated, and the value of the certificate is left to the learner to prove. In late 2021, as the Government Accountability Office began a report on OPMs at the Department of Education's request, 2U announced it would rebrand itself as edX, in an elegant dodge around the inconvenient problem of federal oversight. According to 2U, in an email interview with the edtech journalist Phil Hill, all 3,500 offerings from the joint venture would be offered as edX programs and the remaining partner-facing programs and services would move under the edX brand. Hill wrote, "2U as a brand is not toxic, but it is a target. The rebranding will serve the purpose of leveraging edX's global reach and of changing the perception of 2U's core business and associating it with lower-cost educational offerings."[16]

Coursera Goes Public

On the heels of the pandemic boost in enrollments, Coursera issued an IPO in March 2021. The initial stock price of $33 per share raised about $519 million and gave the company a value of $4.3 billion.[17] At the time, my LinkedIn feed was jammed with friends and former colleagues congratulating the company and each other for making them wealthy. It's easy to see why they were excited: they worked hard for a noble cause—expanding access to education—and became affluent in the process. It's a twenty-first-century dream come true—to do well for yourself while doing good for others—except for the part where a significant portion of the workforce that made the product Coursera sells (university staff) is unrecognized and unrewarded. And also, the product—online courses, certificates, and degrees—mostly reinforces existing power structures in both education and the workforce.

However, while the majority of current and former Coursera employees may have realized a payoff of a few hundred thousand dollars, most are young, paying off student loans, and saving to buy houses or start a family (I did not leave Coursera with shares). Realistically, their shares did not make them wealthy in the Bay Area, where food and shelter are criminally expensive. They were pawns in the start-up game who found themselves on the winning side. The bulk of the Coursera principals who profited most handsomely from this IPO, to the tune of hundreds of millions of dollars, were comfortably multimillionaires *before* Coursera: venture capitalists, the former presidents of Stanford and Yale, tenured professors, and nominally nonprofit institutions that had bought into early investing rounds including Penn, Stanford, and Caltech. True to the financialization of higher education, the most elite people and institutions became more elite—more famous and more wealthy by promising to break down the moats that guard the ivory towers and make education accessible to everyone.

In a sense, both Coursera and edX made good on their initial promise: anyone in the world with access to the internet can now subscribe to an unimaginable set of educational resources and certificates from the best educational brands in the world for as little as $34 a month.[18] Yet even this price, low by U.S. standards, is prohibitive in many countries across the globe.[19] And why have two companies that expanded based on a promise of providing education to the world, including developing countries,[20] ended up serving the same masters and enriching the same people as the universities themselves do?

The Learner Can Be a Winner

Today, anyone with an internet connection can take courses from top institutions for free, or at a very low cost, in topics that are relevant to their interests. Multiple studies show that about three-quarters of learners in the United States who earn a low- or no-cost certificate online from Coursera or edX do experience career benefits, such as learning a new skill, obtaining a new job or role, and learning more about a relevant topic.[21] The top-down approach of highly controlled university degrees is colliding with the bottom-up approach of learner-directed certificates and badges. And while both universities and the federal government have some say in regulating these new credentials, a new arbiter has emerged as well: hiring managers and résumé evaluators. Currently, most human resource professionals generally value degrees more highly than noncredit certificates, and although interest in skills-based digital credentials (sometimes called "microcredentials") is growing, hiring platforms often don't recognize or verify them, so learners don't receive benefit from them.[22]

In 2018, Google launched the Google IT Support Certificate, which provides training in foundational IT skills required for an entry-level job, including customer service, networking, operating systems, and security.[23] One hundred fifty industry partners, including Google, recognize this certificate as a relevant credential for job applicants,[24] and many university systems, including community colleges, grant credit toward a degree for the certificate.[25] The program costs $39 a month (US) and takes approximately six months to complete, but it is also available for free with an application for financial aid. To date, over a million learners have enrolled, 60 percent of whom do not have a college degree. Organizations like Google, IBM, Meta, and HubSpot are now offering certificates that train learners for entry-level roles, and these certificates are now among the most popular on Coursera.[26] On the one hand, these companies are shifting the burden of training from themselves to the potential employee; on the other, they are allowing learners the opportunity to bypass college and gain employment at the largest tech companies in the world. While universities increasingly benefit from rising class anxiety, learners who feel a degree isn't feasible now have a growing set of low-cost, job-relevant educational options that can help promote social mobility. The illusion that universities function as meritocracies that enable social mobility seems to be coming to an end.

Meanwhile, artificial intelligence in education, although slower to develop than in other industries, continued to advance during the pandemic, spurred in part by over $60 million from the National Science Foundation to establish AI institutes in adult learning and online education, student-AI teaming, and engaged learning.[27] Venture capital has backed investments in five main AI capabilities that supported student engagement, learning, personalization, and robotics.[28] Edtech aggregators like Pluralsight, Degreed, and Coursera use algorithms to help create pathways through content for learners who specify a specific learning or career goal. AI was working in the background of education, primarily as a way to enhance and personalize the learning experience—that is, until generative AI was released and ignited a new round of calls for more education, primarily delivered online, to protect workers from being automated out of a job.[29]

The conversational capabilities of Open AI's LLM, ChatGPT,[30] ignited a firestorm of interest, gaining 100 million users in its first two months of availability and $40 billion of venture capital invested in the first half of 2023.[31] Although capabilities were initially seen as a threat to academic integrity, its potential benefits for support, personalization, and assessment also became clear.[32] Universities developed a more measured approach, reflecting on ways to use this new technology to enhance teaching and learning.[33]

What AI in education today promises is personalization to a degree imagined by Pat Suppes almost sixty years ago—an "individual Aristotle" for every student. Other algorithms (some developed at universities but most provided by third-party vendors) are used to identify at-risk students, provide first-level interventions to disengaged or struggling students, and help improve the student experience to be more interactive and engaging, much as Donald Bitzer built in PLATO, but with graphics and sound enabled by today's computing power and technologies and powered by AI algorithms. Papert's student-centered, hands-on, learn-by-doing approach lives on through not only the maker movement in education but also coding bootcamps and the very idea that a learner could build a degree curriculum from the bottom up by stacking relevant certificates to a credential that is recognized by the establishment (even as he disavowed the establishment). In the end, the ideas of Suppes, Bitzer, and Papert are still unfolding into the present and future as computing power and technology are able to realize the vision they set for education over half a century ago. Another touchstone of the early days of CAI—government funding—has also intensified, with the NSF making available $220 million to establish artificial intelligence institutes to "bring about a range of advances" in a number of areas, including a significant investment in learning.[34]

Only a Fool Would Make Predictions, Especially about the Future

—ATTRIBUTED TO SAMUEL GOLDWYN

So now what? The advent of MOOC technology a decade ago (re)ignited the discussion of the effects of technology in education, which has since been influenced by a number of confounding factors including a student loan crisis, the financialization of higher education, income inequality, a stagnation of social mobility not seen since before World War II, a global pandemic, and most recently, generative AI (ChatGPT), which is widely available for free. It is cliché (and a bit of a tautology) to say we are living in unprecedented times. What was certain about edtech in 2021 is uncertain in 2025. Coursera's stock price, which doubled in the first week after its IPO, has yet to stabilize at its initial price of $33 per share.[35] Venture capital funding for edtech reached a peak of nearly US $21 billion globally in 2021 and then plummeted almost 90 percent, with expected investments of only US $580 million during the first quarter of 2024, the lowest rate since 2014.[36] Generative AI seems poised to fundamentally alter teaching and learning, but it's unclear how universities can profit from it, beyond selling online courses on the topic.

In a decade of conversations about the future of higher education and technology at conferences, convenings, hotel lounges, and airport bars with a relatively wonkish rogues' gallery of university vice provosts, edtech CEOs, skeptical professors, digital education administrators, Department of Education staffers, wide-eyed start-up employees, cynical software engineers, and the occasional predatory "vulture capitalist," a few themes converged. Not a single participant in these discussions was naive enough to make any firm predictions about the future of higher education (regardless of the amount of coffee or alcohol consumed and except for the venture capitalists), yet most agreed loosely on the following:

1. In-person learning will remain the gold standard in higher education and will be the province of the undergraduates of elite private institutions. The "elite undergraduate experience" of 2036 will look a lot like it did in

1876, with personal attention from a highly trained instructor being paid to each privileged student.
2. Online learning will become "learning" (modalities will not matter as much as they do today). All learning experiences will be blended to some extent, just as our lives will become increasingly blended between physical and virtual worlds.
3. Universities with significant endowments and brand names will expand their efforts to reach adult students. These big universities will get bigger in terms of the programs they offer and the students they serve but will have to expand their brands to be able to maintain the exclusivity and selectivity of their undergraduate classes while simultaneously attracting adult learners.
4. Nontraditional education providers like Google, IBM, and others will continue to provide pathways to employment that bypass the college degree. Universities will have to differentiate their own offerings and highlight the value of a college degree outside of employability.
5. Organizations will also create training and development pathways for their employees that are personalized and effective and can be recognized by other organizations.
6. Learners will expect to build their own curriculum and get credit toward a degree, just as they will experience personalization (powered by AI) in other areas of their lives.

The future of edtech and higher ed is being written by a small set of remarkably similar people. The vast majority of edtech CEOs, software engineers, venture capitalists, and university vice provosts overseeing digital education—in other words, the decision makers—are fairly homogeneous: educated at name-brand institutions, beneficiaries of the "meritocracy" those institutions provide, genuinely eager to provide access to an education they feel changed their lives. Yet for all their inclusiveness in terms of providing access to digital education, they historically have not provided access to the "room where it happens"— the coffee dates and breakfasts and dinners where decisions are made. What would the future of education look like if there were more diverse voices in the room? Sixty percent of traditional university undergraduates are female, yet only a tiny fraction of those creating the products and the policies that affect these students look like them. The gap between the Ivy league–educated MBAs who lead digital education initiatives and the adult learners they serve is even more stark. The elite are creating the conditions for the non-elite to have access to education in a way that benefits the former more than the latter. Elite institutions benefit socially from making their education available to learners around the globe who could never come to campus, and they benefit financially from investments in those companies that enable the distribution of their assets. But because the universities do not recognize either the certificate as having credit or the learner as a student, those "nontraditional" learners are left on their own to try to turn those certificates into something of value. From a learner's perspective, a noncredit certificate from Google that is recognized by 150 companies may seem like a much better deal.

"History Will Teach Us Nothing"?

—STING

In the midst of the pandemic, two new learning management systems were marketed to universities, Class and Engageli. Both were started by multimillionaire edtech veterans, and both claimed to be inspired by the difficulties faced by their children during homeschooling. Class, founded by Michael Chasen, who is the former CEO and cofounder of Blackboard, "took form at the Chasen kitchen table" after he observed his children receiving remote instruction via Zoom. Profiled in an article in *Forbes*, Chasen is described as "one of the leading voices to pull education back from unknown depths" (the depths are not specified), and Class as "positioned to be the exemplar for an education sector free from the natural tethers of geography and embarking on borderless experiences for teachers and students." The narrative of an entrepreneur rescuing education with technology after having an idea at his kitchen table has certainly resonated with investors. Class has raised over $160 million from investors, including SoftBank, Salesforce, GSV, and Tom Brady.[37]

On the other side of the country, children in another household were "forced to learn using video conferencing tools intended for business meetings." Since the parents of these children were Daphne Koller, cofounder of Coursera, and her husband, Dan Avida, a serial entrepreneur who has made hundreds of millions of dollars from his ventures, they decided to solve the problems of Zoom school because "much worse, for vulnerable populations, the use of these tools led to the loss of critically important years of education." They created Engageli, an edtech platform described in an initial email outreach as "the platform we wish students could have been using in the spring rather than Zoom." She continued, "Somewhat ironically, the interest in using technology to improve the in-class teaching experience was the original impetus that ultimately led me to the founding of Coursera. So Engageli is effectively coming back full circle to my original interests in this space."[38] Engageli has raised $47 million, primarily from private investors in its early rounds of funding.[39] While both Koller and Chasen are right in calling out the learning loss from the sudden switch to remote learning as an important challenge, both assume the solution is through better technology—and investors are following suit. Which begs the question: Why are we so eager to turn to technology to solve educational problems for which the one reliably proven solution is more person-to-person connection?

Because we don't know our own history, and because we do not talk or think about the university as a business, those of us in higher education understand the function of the university in a manner analogous to the parable of the six blind men and the elephant. One blind man, representing, say, the faculty, feels the elephant's trunk and claims it's a snake. Another blind man, representing the students, feels the hide and claims it's a wall. A third, the administrators, hugs the leg and claims it's a tree. And so on. What generally happens in higher education is that five of these blind men (absent the students) convene meetings and fight about which view of higher ed is more important than the others.

Edtech and its venture capital backing, on the other hand, see the whole elephant. And when they describe the elephant to the blind men of the university, they reflect a vision of higher education that benefits their own interests that we accept with less skepticism than we should. For instance, Jeff Maggioncalda, the CEO of Coursera, said in his 2023 conference keynote that "our job collectively, is to make sure we provide more equal access to the knowledge and skills and credentials so that everyone has a chance to get those new opportunities that are being created because of technology."[40] He is not wrong, but he is also not describing the elephant that we are living with—one that provides a high-touch, non-scalable service with intense human interaction that can change the trajectory of someone's life, not just because they learned a new skill but because they developed a new way of thinking about things, or made a new discovery, or trained their brain to wrestle with difficult concepts and complicated ideas. These benefits, which higher ed doesn't do a great job of measuring or promoting, are lost in the vision of the future in which all education is digital, available 24/7 and necessary only insofar as it gets someone to the next job. But if higher ed faculty, administrators, staff, and students keep ourselves in the dark about what higher education does as a business, how it evolved, and where it's going, then we will be at the mercy of those who describe our business to ourselves in ways that serve private equity and billion-dollar endowments and perpetuate the societal inequities we look to higher education to resolve.

Conclusion

Coming Apart at the Polysemes

Education sociologists Charlie Eaton and Mitchell Stevens define the university as "an organization charged with producing, certifying and housing knowledge as embodied in artifacts, practices and human beings (Faculty) and transferring that knowledge across generations through teaching and research training for adults." These functions of producing knowledge, transmitting it (through scholarly publications and teaching), and certifying it (through peer review but also through the conferral of degrees) are what Agarwal was "unbundling" with MOOC technology. But, as Eaton and Stevens point out, the university in U.S. culture is polysemic—meaning it has multiple meanings or can be interpreted in more than one way. U.S. universities can function simultaneously as multibillion-dollar corporations, nonprofits, investment firms, nuclear laboratories, arts centers, hospital systems, real estate investment firms, hospitality centers, and professional-level athletic team owners in addition to their central mission of educating and graduating (aka certifying) four million students per year. Sometimes these various roles (corporation, investment firm, real estate firm) align and sometimes (nonprofit, athletic team owner, educator, and multibillion-dollar corporation) they do not. Further, each institution is culturally unique and resolves the tensions and contradictions in its various roles in its own way.[1]

Despite these differences, there are marked similarities in how universities have responded to educational technology, particularly in how good institutions are at making relatively poor deals with online education platforms, focusing on the wrong risks, and setting up ineffective governance. Even though almost all students from kindergarten through college have taken an online class and/or used educational technology post-Covid, educational institutions encounter difficulties in delivering online programs to the public themselves. Those that eschew OPMs find themselves faced with the increasingly enormous hurdle of trying to market their courses in a crowded and expensive landscape populated by venture-backed start-ups and marketing behemoths like Arizona State University, the University of Phoenix, and Southern New Hampshire University. Until the past decade, universities have been geographic monopolies and have enjoyed the captive markets that resulted. But the advent of new technologies that unbundle the universities' core mission while simultaneously erasing the boundaries of their core markets has destabilized the definition of what the university does even as it has cast a spotlight on the other meanings of the university. "Zoom U" during Covid-19, the Varsity Blues "pay-to-play" admissions scandal, and a heated national debate about student loan debt have many Americans asking, "What is college for? And is it worth it?"[2]

Seven main themes emerged as I was writing and researching this book. Each provides insight into the decisions made by individual professors, corporate executives, and those elected officials who determined research budgets and educational policies. They also reflect a set of collective expectations and convictions that Americans hold about higher education, status, class mobility, and what it means to be educated. Some are more recognizable than others, but all play a significant role in creating the context for higher education in the United States today.

The first, and most foundational theme, is that education is in crisis. In fact, education has always been in crisis since the beginning of the public education system in the United States. This "crisis narrative" is used by politicians, venture capitalists, parents, and students as justification for change of all sorts. The crisis narratives that inform the history of educational technology include: the idea that individual teachers (particularly in K–12) cannot be trusted to teach well and must be held to standards; that lesser-known institutions of higher education don't educate students as well as elite universities; that college costs are "out of control" and college is unaffordable for all but the very wealthy; that what you learn in college is usually irrelevant to what you will be asked to do at work; and that low-cost, high-quality education (from elite institutions) will solve a host of social ills both in the United States and abroad. Many of these crisis narratives are evergreen—persisting across decades, and now deeply embedded in how we think about education and what "problems" we choose to solve.

And many of the crisis narratives we accept as truth rely on the foundational assumption of hierarchy in higher education, specifically that elite institutions not only are better at educating students but also have capabilities far beyond their scope, such as supporting globalization and promoting democracy. This second theme manifests as follows: we do not question that a

Stanford or Harvard education is "better" than the education at a small liberal arts college, a state school, or a community college. One reason this assumption persists is that we easily equate status with quality: Yale graduates must be better educated than those from the City College of New York. Yet one of the only obvious differences between the two sets of graduates is earning power and representation in "elite" job fields such as consulting, private equity, and university faculty. Those who benefit from this assumption include every graduate of an elite university (myself included), the universities themselves, which can charge a premium in tuition, private equity firms that make money investing university endowments and collect a portion of the profits as bonuses, and venture capital firms that monetize "democratizing education" by investing in educational technology that distributes education from elite institutions to anyone with an internet connection for a fee, among others.

The idea that education is a poorly run business is a third theme. As I discovered, this theme is rooted in reality; at the same time, it also enables a host of assumptions that educational technology firms of today exploit, including the idea that efficiency in education is a desired state. The notion that education should be more efficient motivated the earliest experiments in "teaching machines" in the early 1920s and continues to do so today. This idea persists in spite of the consistent findings from both research and practitioners' and most students' personal experience that the inefficiencies of higher education—the time- and resource-intensive interactions between teachers and learners and learners with each other—are most likely to create meaningful learning experiences. On the other hand, universities can be highly inefficient bureaucracies that create the conditions for their own disruption through disdain of business, distrust of innovation, and a dangerously nostalgic view (often held by faculty) that multimillion- if not multibillion-dollar organizations are best run by academics with no prior business experience.

Yet disruption would not be possible without the hacker ethic, the fourth theme. Born at MIT in the late 1950s and early 1960s, the hacker ethic presumes that disruption is always positive, information should always be free, and authority is untrustworthy. Most importantly for this book, hackers believe that formal education can get in the way of true genius, can stifle creativity, and is practiced by uninformed, unimaginative, yet well-meaning teachers. Most educational technology is built on the idea that education needs to be reformed (crisis narrative), that technology-enabled disruption will make education better: that is, more easily accessible, higher quality, and less expensive, and that those who resist the disruption are doomed to repeat ineffective and expensive practices. Because the hacker ethic is closely knitted with technology disruption, the two are often viewed as synonymous, especially in higher education.[3]

The clash between the ideals of hacker ethic/technology disruption and the ideals of university culture is the fifth theme. Universities take their time, move slowly, and resist change. Hackers were born out of this culture and are always in resistance to it; therefore, the two can never align in any meaningful sense. The tension between the two cultures is a gold mine for venture capitalists who back educational technology ventures, including online program managers (OPMs). And when universities look to engage with edtech, their high level of risk aversion encourages a "buy as a pack" mentality. This behavior has been exploited by businesses beyond edtech, and it has led to practices such as preferential contracts and guaranteed payments for brand-name institutions in order to generate both credibility and urgency in the buying process for the broader university market. Thus, there is a clear financial incentive to keep educational technology separate from the university. For the more incomprehensible, foreign, and disruptive an educational technology such as online learning is, the greater the opportunity to sell services that promise to tame it in service of the university. And if Harvard, Princeton, and the University of Michigan are using these services, then other universities are likely to buy in without as much due diligence.

The "golden wedge" between universities and educational technology capitalizes on the sixth theme, the "unbundling" of higher education. The metaphor of unbundling itself is deeply rooted in a technological mindset, given that a bundle is made up of a set of discrete objects that can be disaggregated, similar to the framework used in programming languages. Every time a higher education practice (say, delivering lectures or grading assignments) is extracted from the many roles a university plays, that extracted practice can be automated, scaled, and monetized—all of which rely upon standardization. Yet standardization results in the loss of individuality, and so "unbundled" university practices are removed from the unique culture of each institution, thereby putting pressure on non-scalable practices (career advising, alumni networks, small group discussion, etc.) to carry the weight of the institution's identity. And non-scalable, unique interactions, what are often referred to as "high-touch" interactions, are increasingly expensive to provide.

Finally, the upward spiral of both tuition costs and university endowments underscores almost every aspect of this research, from crisis narratives (college costs too much, student loans are out of control) to business practices (universities waste money by being inefficient) to the quality of education (higher tuition signals better education). Often ignored is the role that universities play in venture capital funding and the profits a select few make from educational technology. Ivy League universities have been investing in venture capital funds through their endowments since the 1970s. Stanford University in particular has a very porous border between venture capital and its leadership. But today, almost every elite institution in the United States has endowment investments in private equity, whose profits are generated in part from tuition dollars collected by for-profit universities and online program managers. Educational technology developed at elite institutions has not only enriched a few professors and venture capital investors but also benefited universities themselves through their endowments and also through direct investments (although these are a very small fraction of any university investment portfolio). For example, the University of Pennsylvania, Caltech, Stanford, and others were early investors in Coursera, and Harvard and MIT received $800 million for edX. The degree to which elite institutions have profited from educational technology, whether it be financially, in brand expansion, in generating goodwill, or in burnishing their reputations as "innovators," is significant. And yet the success of these technological innovations is reliant upon ignorance of their history, including evidence-based research of their effectiveness.

The Violence of Forgetting

Would universities purchase, use, or enter into contracts with edtech companies and participate in this new education marketplace if they knew that their ideas of expanding education with computer technologies were recycled? We may never know the answer, since it is unlikely that even the latest technological advances will cause universities to suddenly become aware that over half a century ago, they participated in nationally funded experiments in educational technology that were seen as a tool for foreign policy and domestic security.

And almost no one in the business of making educational technologies is aware that its history of educational technology is intertwined with the history of artificial intelligence, the history of student loans, and the history of the post–World War II university in the United States. Only a few sociologists and cultural critics have woven the disparate threads of technology, educational entrepreneurship, foreign and domestic governmental policies, market opportunities, and regulation to form a richer tapestry of understanding the forces behind online learning's origins and adoption. Some scholars go so far as to argue that the United States "embraces a mode of historical amnesia 'in which forgetting has become more important than learning'"[4] so that the public can be sold ideas (like the education gospel, and higher education as an investment in future earnings) that profit the already privileged and wealthy.

On a practical level, if higher education is aware of the history of its own technological "disruptions," then we can be more informed consumers of educational technology, more prepared to partner with platforms, more clear-eyed about what "disruption" is and where it is happening, and ultimately less subject to the influence of the homogeneous higher ed "disrupters"— those thought leaders, administrators, and entrepreneurs who preach the gospel of technological change to higher ed administration and federal policymakers while obfuscating financial motives and measurement of results. Being more informed about higher ed's technological history also empowers us to escape what Seymour Papert called "The QWERTY trap" of allowing technology to determine our behavior instead of letting our behavior determine the technology. And finally, by understanding the forces that come together to enable the creation of technology, we can better understand that technology alone is not that powerful. Instead, its power is derived from an assemblage of political, governmental, social, and cultural forces. In most cases, what we call technology is a symptom of issues in education, not what ails it. And ultimately, it is a force we can use—and must use, for the good of students everywhere.

My sincerest hope is that this book will help shed some light on this hidden, forgotten history.

ACKNOWLEDGMENTS

Peter Dougherty asked me to lunch and somehow I ended up writing a book proposal. This was not the purpose of the lunch. His clear vision and steadfast belief in this project propelled it through stormy conditions (including a pandemic, a job change, the collapse of the edtech market, Peter's retirement, and a crippling case of imposter syndrome). The book would not exist without his stewardship and friendship.

Matt Rohal at Princeton University Press inherited this project and immediately adopted it as his own. His incisive editing, guidance, patience, and kindness were invaluable. Alena Chekanov shepherded the manuscript through the many stages to publication with great expertise. Thanks also to Jenn Backer and Nathan Carr for turning a massive Word document into a book.

Rachel Kolbin is one of the best writing teachers and coaches anyone could have. Sometimes, it's enough to write one sentence a day. Thank you for slogging through the earliest draft with me.

Roger Schonfeld and Jenny Stine read the "not ready for primetime" draft and gave crucial suggestions for making it better. Marc Sanders and Piotr Mitros graciously walked down memory lane with me to give added insight to the MOOC chapters. Mitchell Stevens elevated this manuscript, not once, but twice, by asking all the right questions and encouraging new avenues of inquiry.

It is an odd and challenging experience to write a history that you helped create. First at Stanford, then at Coursera, NovoEd, Wharton, and the Sands Institute for Lifelong Learning at UVA Darden, my colleagues and I learned that when you invent new solutions to educational access, you also invent new problems. Thanks to all of you for the many, many hours devoted to creating new forms of education for new kinds of learners, and for believing it is a worthwhile pursuit. Thank you also to the scholars who provide sorely needed research into the effectiveness and the effects of these technologies on learners. Though most of you will never give a TED Talk on disrupting education, your work deserves millions of views.

Jeff Himpele has been a part of every stage of this process, from advising on drafts of the proposal, to reading chapters out of order, to patiently listening to me question, kvetch, complain, and talk my way into understanding what I wanted to say. Your love and support have made me a book author, a better thinker, and a nicer human being.

I took the job at Stanford because I was a new mother and needed flexible hours. I took the job at Coursera because I was a newly single mother and needed to jump-start my career. My deepest thanks go to my son, Liam, who played in the other room while I was teaching, who slept on the floor at Coursera, who figured out how to take an Uber home from Little League when I was stuck on the 101 coming back from NovoEd, who did his homework after school at Wharton, and who moved every time I got a new job. Thank you for always waiting for me at pick-up and for liking takeout dinners. Our family will always be my favorite start-up.

HOW I WROTE THIS BOOK

NOTES ON SOURCES

The Teacher in the Machine was conceptualized as a history of online education written from a combination of primary and secondary sources with a sprinkling of personal experience. For the events prior to 2004, I turned to primary sources whenever possible, including oral histories, personal archives, magazines, newspapers, government reports, advertisements, and scholarly articles written by the subjects themselves. The Charles Babbage Institute Archives at the University of Minnesota is an incredible trove of personal recollections, as are the Stanford Oral History collections. The secondary sources included some invaluable historical accounts. Of special note were Brian Dear's *The Friendly Orange Glow* on the history of PLATO, Audrey Watters's *Teaching Machines* on the inventions of Pressey and Skinner, Katie Hafner's *Where Wizards Stay Up Late* on the origins of the internet, Annalee Saxenian's *Regional Advantage: Culture and Competition in Silicon Valley and Route 128* on the social and cultural differences between Stanford and MIT, and Margaret O'Mara's *The Code* on the history of Silicon Valley.

I took a job as a human in the loop for Pat Suppes at Stanford in 2004. Since then, I have worked for and with many of the people, organizations, and institutions covered in this book, which are listed at the end of this essay. Many of the primary sources in the second half include a mix of formal interviews, conference presentations, formal convenings, and meetings as well as informal conversations in the course of "doing business" in online education over the past two decades. Since I work in academia, many of my colleagues who are faculty have produced important research about the effectiveness of online education and adaptive tutoring, including Ryan Baker, Carolyn Rose, Fiona Hollands, Rene Kizilcec, George Siemens, David Joyner, Paolo Blikstein, Christopher Brooks, Justin Reich, Rebecca Eynon, Miggy Andres-Bray, Elle Wang, and Ken Koedinger. Their research not only provides the foundation for understanding how students can engage with online learning environments but also has guided the design and development of many online educational programs. Some notable secondary sources specifically on the recent history of online education are: Justin Reich's *Failure to Disrupt: Why Technology Alone Can't Transform Education*, Taylor Walsh's *Unlocking the Gates: How and Why Leading Universities Are Opening Up Access to Their Courses* on elite universities' initial forays into online education, and Larry Cuban's *The Flight of a Butterfly or the Path of a Bullet? Using Technology to Transform Teaching and Learning*.

The initial plan for this book described a chronological history of online education from its inception in the late 1950s through the MOOC craze of 2012 and the rise of online program managers (OPMs). Since I began writing in 2019, there has been a pandemic, which led to almost every school in the United States, from kindergarten to graduate school, offering online instruction, investment funding for edtech spiking and then cratering, a massive loss of trust in higher education, the advent of ChatGPT, and, as I write this, a new call for AI to "revolutionize education." The pace of change is so fast that my son, who was in third grade when the first video and MOOCs revolution was going to "totally disrupt" education, is still in school as a college undergraduate during a second education revolution of his young lifetime. My efforts to understand why these revolutions keep happening and why we are supposed to accept that we need revolutions in the first place led me to some amazing writers and scholars whose work on the financial, cultural, social, and governmental forces that create the conditions for these revolutions should be on everyone's reading list. They include: Charlie Eaton, *Bankers in the Ivory Tower*; Morgan Ames, *The Charisma Machine*; Richard Ohmann and Ira Shor, *Is College Worth It? Class and the Myth of the College Premium*; Louis Menand, *The Marketplace of Ideas*; and Tressie McMillan Cottom, *Lower Ed: The Troubling Rise of For-Profit Colleges in the New Economy*. Alexander Kindel and Mitchell L. Stevens's article, "What Is Educational Entrepreneurship? Strategic Action, Temporality, and the Expansion of US Higher Education," provided the framework for this book and should be widely read for understanding the sociocultural motivations of universities in engaging with technology to reach nontraditional students and partner with industry.

The following individuals have deepened my understanding of online education and educational technology, some through formal interviews (marked by an asterisk), others in informal conversations at conferences or at work.

Jeremy Adelman, Princeton University
Anant Agarwal, edX
Bharat Anad, Harvard Business School
Ryan Baker, University of Pennsylvania
Randy Bass, Georgetown University

Leah Belsky, Coursera
Relly Brandman, Coursera
Anthony Bryk, Carnegie Foundation for the Advancement of Teaching and Learning
Peter Capelli, University of Pennsylvania
Julia Dallos, Coursera
Brian Dear, author, *The Friendly Orange Glow**
Ashwin Demara, Emeritus
Ellen Desmaris, Harvard Business Publishing
James DeVaney, University of Michigan*
Yasmin Kafai, University of Pennsylvania
Jon Katzman, Noodle
Mona Fixdal, Princeton University
Geoff Garrett, University of Pennsylvania, University of Southern California
Jamal Gay, Noodle
James Hilton, University of Virginia, University of Michigan
Jeffrey Himpele, Princeton University
Fiona Hollands, Columbia University
Gautam Kaul, University of Michigan
Rene Kizilcec, Cornell University
Pang Wei Koh, Coursera
Daphne Koller, Coursera
Clint Korver, Ulu Ventures
Hunt Lambert, Harvard University
Sharon Leu, Department of Education
Rick Levin, Coursera
Jia Lu, Coursera
Rob Lue, Harvard University
Rob Magliaro, Grow with Google
Mike Malefakis, University of Pennsylvania*

Rafe Mazzeo, Stanford University*
John Mitchell, Stanford University
Ted Mitchell, Department of Education
Piotr Mitros, edX
Patrick Mullane, Harvard Business School
Andrew Ng, Coursera
Jiquan Niam, Coursera
Vincent Price, University of Pennsylvania, Duke University
Kathy Pugh, edX
Lou Pugliese, New Market Ventures, Ashford University, Blackboard*
Deanna Rainieri, Coursera
Jagmohan Raju, University of Pennsylvania
Matthew Rascoff, University of North Carolina, Duke University, Stanford University
Ray Ravaglia, Stanford University, OHS
Farnaz Ronaghi, Stanford University, NovoEd
Carolyn Rose, Carnegie Mellon University
Amin Saberi, Stanford University, NovoEd
Marc Sanders, Stanford University, EPGY, OHS*
Sreecharan Sankaranarayanan, Carnegie Mellon University
Matt Sigelman, Burning Glass Institute
Nicolaj Siggelkow, University of Pennsylvania
Himanshu Singh, Coursera
Nikhil Sinha, Coursera
Bob Smith, Stanford University, EPGY
Nancy Smith, Stanford University, EPGY
David Soo, Department of Education*
Mitchell Stevens, Stanford University
Julia Stiglitz, Coursera
Jenny Stine, MIT*
Patrick Suppes, Stanford University*

Christian Tierwich, University of Pennsylvania
Karl Ulrich, University of Pennsylvania
Toby Wall, MIT*
Emily Whelan, Coursera
Jason Wingard, Columbia University

Thank you all. It's been a hell of a ride.

NOTES

Introduction

1. Justin Reich, *Failure to Disrupt: Why Technology Alone Can't Transform Education* (Cambridge, MA: Harvard University Press, 2020).

2. Audrey Watters, *Teaching Machines: The History of Personalized Learning* (Cambridge, MA: MIT Press, 2021).

3. E. J. Emanuel, "MOOCs Taken by Educated Few," *Nature* 503, no. 7476 (2013): 342.

4. Margaret O'Mara, *The Code: Silicon Valley and the Remaking of America* (New York: Penguin, 2020), 400.

5. Charlie Eaton, *Bankers in the Ivory Tower: The Troubling Rise of Financiers in US Higher Education* (Chicago: University of Chicago Press, 2022).

6. Tressie McMillan Cottom, *Lower Ed: The Troubling Rise of For-profit Colleges in the New Economy* (New York: New Press, 2017).

7. Seymour A. Papert, *Mindstorms: Children, Computers, and Powerful Ideas* (New York: Basic Books, 1980), 5.

8. Alexander T. Kindel and Mitchell L. Stevens, "What Is Educational Entrepreneurship? Strategic Action, Temporality, and the Expansion of US Higher Education," *Theory and Society* 50 (2021): 577–605, 577.

9. https://www.mheducation.com/prek-12/explore/redbird/language-arts-writing.html.

10. https://ohs.stanford.edu/.

11. John Markoff, "Patrick Suppes, Pioneer in Computerized Learning, Dies at 92," *New York Times*, December 2, 2014, https://www.nytimes.com/2014/12/03/us/patrick-suppes-pioneer-in-computerized-learning-dies-at-92.html.

12. https://www.youtube.com/watch?v=nTFEUsudhfs.

13. "Ed Tech Pulls in $1.1B of Funding in 2012. Top 10 Deals Take 1/3 of Funding. There Is No Ed Tech Bubble," CBInsights, January 21, 2013, https://www.cbinsights.com/research/ed-tech-deals-bubble/.

14. Michael Noer, "One Man, One Computer, 10 Million Students: How Khan Academy Is Reinventing Education," *Forbes*, November 2, 2012, https://www.forbes.com/sites/michaelnoer/2012/11/02/one-man-one-computer-10-million-students-how-khan-academy-is-reinventing-education/?sh=2ef48fd744e0.

15. "Much of what Khan Academy discovered by 2019 about computer-assisted math instruction, after more than $100 million in philanthropic investment, could have been found in academic papers published in the 1990s." Reich, *Failure to Disrupt*, 6.

16. Sal Kahn, "How AI Could Save (Not Destroy) Education," https://www.youtube.com/watch?v=hJP5GqnTrNo.

17. B. Williamson, A. Molnar, and F. Boninger, *Time for a Pause: Without Effective Public Oversight, AI in Schools Will Do More Harm than Good* (Boulder, CO: National Education Policy Center, 2024), http://nepc.colorado.edu/publication/ai.

18. Matt Barnum, "We Tested an AI Tutor for Kids. It Struggled with Basic Math," *Wall Street Journal*, February 16, 2024, https://www.wsj.com/tech/ai/ai-is-tutoring-students-but-still-struggles-with-basic-math-694e76d3.

19. P. T. von Hippel, "Two-Sigma Tutoring: Separating Science Fiction from Science Fact," *Education Next* 24, no. 2 (2024): 22–31.

20. https://projects.propublica.org/nonprofits/organizations/261544963.

21. Kate Stoltzfus, "Paul Tough on Fixing Higher Education's Broken System," ACSD, May 1, 2022, https://www.ascd.org/el/articles/paul-tough-on-fixing-higher-educations-broken-system.

Chapter 1: The Men behind the Curtain

1. https://www.youtube.com/watch?v=Q1MMM4UKn5w.

2. See Larry Cuban, *The Flight of a Butterfly or the Path of a Bullet? Using Technology to Transform Teaching and Learning* (Cambridge, MA: Harvard Education Press, 2018); Justin Reich, *Failure to Disrupt: Why Technology Alone Can't Transform Education* (Cambridge, MA: Harvard University Press, 2020).

3. https://finance.yahoo.com/news/edtech-market-size-grow-usd-081700278.html.

4. U.S. Senate, "Sputnik Spurs Passage of the National Defense Education Act," October 4, 1957, https://www.senate.gov/artandhistory/history/minute/Sputnik_Spurs_Passage_of_National_Defense_Education_Act.htm.

5. Cuban, *The Flight of a Butterfly or the Path of a Bullet*, 124.

6. National Research Council, *Funding a Revolution: Government Support for Computing Research* (Washington, DC: National Academies Press, 1999), https://doi.org/10.17226/6323.

7. "PLATO and the Genesis of Computer Learning," *Limitless Magazine*, University of Illinois, https://grainger.illinois.edu/news/magazine/plato.

8. Audrey Watters, "Teaching Machines and Turing Machines: The History of the Future of Labor and Learning" https://hackeducation.com/2015/08/10/digpedlab.

9. Sheelagh Drudy, "Gender Balance/Gender Bias: The Teaching Profession and the Impact of Feminisation," *Gender and Education* 20, no. 4 (2008): 309–23.

10. Audrey Watters, *Teaching Machines: The History of Personalized Learning* (Cambridge, MA: MIT Press, 2021).

11. L. T. Benjamin, "A History of Teaching Machines," *American Psychologist* 43, no. 9 (1988): 703.

12. B. F. Skinner, "Baby in a Box," *Ladies Home Journal* 62, no. 10 (1945): 30–31.

13. A. Rutherford, *Beyond the Box: BF Skinner's Technology of Behaviour from Laboratory to Life, 1950s–1970s* (Toronto: University of Toronto Press, 2009).

14. B. F. Skinner, "Teaching Machines," *Science* (October 24, 1958): 969–77, 977.

15. B. F. Skinner, "Teaching Machines," *Scientific American* 205, no. 5 (1961): 90–106.

16. Watters, *Teaching Machines*.

17. Cuthbert C. Hurd, interview by Nancy Stern, January 20, 1981, "An Interview with Cuthbert C. Hurd," OH 76, Charles Babbage Institute, Center for the History of Information Processing, University of Minnesota.

18. Hurd, interview.

19. Eugene Galanter, *Automatic Teaching: The State of the Art* (New York: John Wiley and Sons, 1959), 1.

20. Galanter, *Automatic Teaching*, 4.

21. Galanter, *Automatic Teaching*, 3.

22. J. Rath Gustave, Nancy S. Anderson, and R. C. Brainers, "The IBM Research Teaching Machine Project," in Eugene Galanter, *Automatic Teaching: The State of the Art* (New York: John Wiley and Sons, 1959), 126.

23. Galanter, *Automatic Teaching*.

24. William J. Carr, *Self-Instructional Devices: A Review of Current Concepts* (Wright-Patterson Air Force Base, OH: Air Force Human Resources Lab, 1959), 3, 4, 19.

25. U.S. Senate, "Sputnik Spurs Passage of the National Defense Education Act."

26. M. L. Stevens and B. Gebre-Medhin, "Association, Service, Market: Higher Education in American Political Development," *Annual Review of Sociology* 42 (2016): 121–42.

27. Marvin Minsky, interview by Arthur L. Norberg, November 1, 1989, "An Interview with Marvin Minsky," OH 179, Charles Babbage Institute, Center for the History of Information Processing, University of Minnesota.

28. Andrew Molnar and Beverly Sherman, *U.S. Office of Education Support of Computer Activities* (Washington, DC: Office of Education, 1969).

29. Thomas Gallie, interview by William Aspray, November 1990, "An Interview with Thomas Gallie," Charles Babbage Institute, Center for the History of Information Processing, University of Minnesota.

30. Andrew Molnar, interview by William Aspray, September 25, 1991, "Andrew R. Molnar: An Oral History," Charles Babbage Institute, University of Minnesota, https://conservancy.umn.edu/items/a6d46f50-8bed-4a3e-aded-9d285759349d.

31. Gallie, interview.

32. Edward Feigenbaum, interview by Pamela McCorduck, June 12, 1979, "An Interview with Edward Feigenbaum," OH 14, Charles Babbage Institute, Center for the History of Information Processing, University of Minnesota.

33. P. Suppes and M. Jerman, "Computer Assisted Instruction at Stanford," *Educational Technology* 9, no. 1 (1969): 22–24.

34. Minsky, interview.

35. Seymour Papert, *Mindstorms: Children, Computers, and Powerful Ideas* (New York: Basic Books, 1980), 33.

Chapter 2: Experimenting for the Future

The epigraph comes from: Andrew Molnar, interview by William Aspray, September 25, 1991, "Andrew R. Molnar: An Oral History"; Andrew Molnar, "Computers in Education: A Brief History," *THE Journal*, June 1, 1997, https://thejournal.com/articles/1997/06/01/computers-in-education-a-brief-history.aspx.

1. Seymour Papert, *Mindstorms: Children, Computers, and Powerful Ideas* (New York: Basic Books, 1980), 157.

2. Bob Johnstone, *Never Mind the Laptops: Kids, Computers, and the Transformation of Learning* (Lincoln, NE: iUniverse, 2003).

3. Marvin Minsky, interview by Arthur L. Norberg, November 1, 1989, "An Interview with Marvin Minsky," OH 179, Charles Babbage Institute, Center for the History of Information Processing, University of Minnesota.

4. Gary Stager, "Seymour Papert (1928–2016)," *Nature* (September 14, 2016): 308.

5. Seymour Papert and Cynthia Solomon, "Twenty Things to Do with a Computer," Artificial Intelligence Memo Number 248 (Cambridge, MA: MIT, 1971).

6. Papert, *Mindstorms*, 177.

7. Papert, *Mindstorms*, 5.

8. Johnstone, *Never Mind the Laptops*.

9. Papert, *Mindstorms*, 7.

10. Edith Ackermann, "Piaget's Constructivism, Papert's Constructionism: What's the Difference?" *Future of Learning Group Publication* 5, no. 3 (2001): 438.

11. Papert, *Mindstorms*, 8.

12. Papert, *Mindstorms*, 36–37.

13. Patrick Suppes, "Memories and Fantasies of my Intellectual Autobiography (1 of 2)," https://web.stanford.edu/group/cslipublications/cslipublications/SuppesCorpus/lectures.html.

14. Patrick Suppes, interview by David Mitchell, 2007, Patrick Suppes, Stanford Historical Society Oral History Program Interviews (SC0932).

15. Patrick Suppes, "The Uses of Computers in Education," *Scientific American* (September 1, 1966): 207–20, 219.

16. Suppes, interview.

17. "Professor John McCarthy: Father of AI," jmc.stanford.edu.

18. Suppes, interview.

19. Suppes, "The Uses of Computers in Education," 207–8.

20. Anne Trumbore, "Automated and Amplified," *Historical Instructional Design Cases: ID Knowledge in Context and Practice* (2020): 134.

21. Patrick Suppes, "Patrick Suppes Intellectual Biography," Patrick Suppes Corpus, n.d., https://suppes-corpus.stanford.edu/.

22. D. L. Bitzer, E. R. Lyman, and J. A. Easley Jr., "The Uses of PLATO: A Computer-Controlled Teaching System," Coordinated Science Laboratory Report no. R-268 (1965), 7.

23. Bitzer, Lyman, and Easley, "The Uses of PLATO," 14.

24. Donald Bitzer, interview by Sheldon Hocheiser, 1988, Charles Babbage Institute, Center for the History of Information Processing, University of Minnesota.

25. Using PLATO IV ERIC Number: ED124144.

26. https://archon.library.illinois.edu/archives/index.php?p=creators/creator&id=123.

27. Thomas Gallie, interview by William Aspray, 1990, Charles Babbage Institute, Center for the History of Information Processing, University of Minnesota.

28. D. Alpert and D. L. Bitzer, "Advances in Computer-Based Education: The Plato Program Will Provide a Major Test of the Educational and Economic Feasibility of This Medium," *Science* 167, no. 3925 (1970): 1582–90, 1583.

29. Using PLATO IV ERIC Number: ED124144.

30. https://archon.library.illinois.edu/archives/index.php?p=creators/creator&id=123.

31. https://www.nsf.gov/nsb/documents/2000/nsb00215/nsb50/1970/mansfield.html.

32. https://umsi580.lsait.lsa.umich.edu/s/PLATOs-Citizens/page/welcome.
33. Suppes, interview.
34. Johnstone, *Never Mind the Laptops*, 42.
35. Johnstone, *Never Mind the Laptops*.
36. Seymour Papert and Cynthia Solomon, "Twenty Things to Do with a Computer," Artificial Intelligence Memo Number 248 (Cambridge, MA: MIT, 1971), 30–31.
37. Papert, *Mindstorms*, 215.

Chapter 3: Commercialization

1. Bob Smith, CCC Reunion Dinner, 2015, https://www.youtube.com/watch?v=Q1MMM4UKn5w.
2. Kathryn Harris, "Taking a Megabyte of the Market: Technology: Computer Curriculum Has Seen Its Growth Explode as Classrooms Go Multimedia," *Los Angeles Times*, March 18, 1993, https://www.latimes.com/archives/la-xpm-1993-03-18-fi-12443-story.html.
3. Lego Mindstorms 2020, https://www.fatbraintoys.com/toy_companies/lego_systems_inc/lego_mindstorms_2020.cfm?country=US.
4. M. L. Stevens and B. Gebre-Medhin, "Association, Service, Market: Higher Education in American Political Development," *Annual Review of Sociology* 42 (2016): 121–42.
5. Charlie Eaton, *Bankers in the Ivory Tower: The Troubling Rise of Financiers in US Higher Education* (Chicago: University of Chicago Press, 2022), 40.
6. L. T. Hamilton and K. Nielsen, *Broke: The Racial Consequences of Underfunding Public Universities* (Chicago: University of Chicago Press, 2021), 201.
7. Marvin Minsky and Seymour A. Papert, *Perceptron: An Introduction to Computational Geometry* (Cambridge, MA: MIT Press 1969), 1–2.
8. James Lighthill, "Artificial Intelligence: A General Survey," in *Artificial Intelligence: A Paper Symposium* (London: Science Research Council, 1973), 1–21.
9. J. Agar, "What Is Science For? The Lighthill Report on Artificial Intelligence Reinterpreted," *British Journal for the History of Science* 53, no. 3 (2020): 289–310.
10. Marvin Minsky and Seymour A. Papert, *Perceptrons: An Introduction to Computational Geometry*, rev. ed. (Cambridge, MA: MIT Press, 2017), x.
11. Alexander T. Kindel and Mitchell L. Stevens, "What Is Educational Entrepreneurship? Strategic Action, Temporality, and the Expansion of US Higher Education," *Theory and Society* 50 (2021): 577–605.
12. Patrick Suppes, "Patrick Suppes Intellectual Biography," p. 37, Patrick Suppes Corpus, n.d., https://suppes-corpus.stanford.edu/.

13. Ron Fortune, CCC Reunion Dinner, 2015, https://www.youtube.com/watch?v=Q1MMM4UKn5w.

14. Jeffrey Tlumak, ed., *Newsletter on Teaching Philosophy* (American Philosophical Association, 1980), 6–9.

15. Patrick Suppes and Stanford University, *University-Level, Computer-Assisted Instruction at Stanford, 1968–1980* (Stanford, CA: Institute for Mathematical Studies in the Social Sciences, 1981), xxxii.

16. Patrick Suppes and R. Smith, "Computers in Education: A Half-century of Innovation" (Center for the Study of Language and Information, 2017), 77. Note that the telephones students used were heavy, desktop landlines and therefore difficult to hurl across the room in frustration.

17. Anne Trumbore, "Automated and Amplified," *Historical Instructional Design Cases: ID Knowledge in Context and Practice* (2020): 134, 136.

18. Trumbore, "Automated and Amplified."

19. B. Dear, personal communication with the author, November 11, 2021.

20. Donald Bitzer, interview by Sheldon Hocheiser, 1988, Charles Babbage Institute, Center for the History of Information Processing, University of Minnesota.

21. Bitzer, interview.

22. G. Slattow, "Demonstration of the PLATO IV Computer-Based Education System. Final Report. January 1, 1972–June 30, 1976," Computer-Based Education Research Laboratory, University of Illinois, 1977, https://eric.ed.gov/?id=ED158767.

23. Bitzer, interview.

24. Andrew Pollack, "An Era Ends at Control Data," *New York Times*, January 11, 1986, https://www.nytimes.com/1986/01/11/business/an-era-ends-at-control-data.html.

25. Brian Dear, *The Friendly Orange Glow: The Untold Story of the PLATO System and the Dawn of Cyberculture* (New York: Random House, 2017).

26. Dear, *The Friendly Orange Glow*, 499.

27. Gary S. Stager, "Seymour Papert (1928–2016)," *Nature* 537, no. 7620 (2016): 308.

28. Gary S. Stager, "The Daily Papert: About," https://dailypapert.com/about/.

29. Morgan Ames, *The Charisma Machine: The Life, Death, and Legacy of One Laptop per Child* (Cambridge, MA: MIT Press, 2019), 2.

30. Seymour Papert, *Mindstorms: Children, Computers, and Powerful Ideas* (New York: Basic Books, 1980).

31. Cynthia Solomon et al., "History of Logo," *Proceedings of the ACM on Programming Languages* 4, HOPL (2020): 1–66.

32. P. Boytchev, "Logo Tree Project," October 2014, https://web.archive.org/web/20180820132053/http://elica.net:80/download/papers/LogoTreeProject.pdf.

33. A. L. Duckworth, C. Peterson, M. D. Matthews, and D. R. Kelly, "Grit: Perseverance and Passion for Long-term Goals," *Journal of Personality and Social Psychology* 92, no. 6 (2007): 1087.

34. Ames, *The Charisma Machine*.

35. R. D. Pea and D. M. Kurland, "On the Cognitive Effects of Learning Computer Programming," *New Ideas in Psychology* 2, no. 2 (1984): 137–68.

36. P. Connolly, C. Keenan, and K. Urbanska, "The Trials of Evidence-Based Practice in Education: A Systematic Review of Randomised Controlled Trials in Education Research, 1980–2016," *Educational Research* 60, no. 3 (2018): 276–91.

37. Seymour Papert, "Information Technology and Education: Computer Criticism vs. Technocentric Thinking," *Educational Researcher* 16, no. 1 (1987): 22–30, 26.

38. https://www.media.mit.edu/about/history/.

39. E. G. Coleman and A. Golub, "Hacker Practice: Moral Genres and the Cultural Articulation of Liberalism," *Anthropological Theory* 8, no. 3 (2008): 255–77.

40. Morgan G. Ames, "Hackers, Computers, and Cooperation: A Critical History of Logo and Constructionist Learning," *Proceedings of the ACM on Human-Computer Interaction* 2, no. CSCW (2018): 1–19, https://dl.acm.org/doi/10.1145/3274287.

41. Morgan G. Ames and Daniela K. Rosner, "From Drills to Laptops: Designing Modern Childhood Imaginaries," *Information, Communication & Society* 17, no. 3 (2014): 357–70.

42. Laura Pappano, "The Boy Genius of Ulan Bator," *New York Times*, September 13, 2013, https://www.nytimes.com/2013/09/15/magazine/the-boy-genius-of-ulan-bator.html.

43. Ames, *The Charisma Machine*.

44. Mark Warschauer and Morgan Ames, "Can One Laptop per Child Save the World's Poor?" *Journal of International Affairs* (2010): 33–51, 46.

45. https://ocw.mit.edu/about/.

46. C. M. Stracke, S. Downes, G. Conole, D. Burgos, and F. Nascimbeni, "Are MOOCs Open Educational Resources? A Literature Review on History, Definitions and Typologies of OER and MOOCs," *Open Praxis* 11, no. 4 (2019): 331–41.

47. Patrick Suppes and Robert Smith, *Computers in Education: A Half-Century of Innovation* (Center for the Study of Language and Information, 2017), 265.

48. Patrick Suppes, interview by David Mitchell, 2007, Patrick Suppes, Stanford Historical Society Oral History Program Interviews (SC0932).

49. Suppes and Smith, *Computers in Education*, 242–62.

50. Suppes, interview.

51. Suppes and Smith, *Computers in Education*, 264.

52. Suppes and Smith, *Computers in Education*, 265.

53. https://www.businessinsider.com/smartest-private-high-schools-in-the-us-2015-3#6-stanford-online-high-school--stanford-california-45.

54. Patrick Suppes, interview, in Luciano Floridi, ed., *Philosophy of Computing and Information, 5 Questions* (Copenhagen: Automatic Press/VIP, 2008), 141–57, 149.

55. https://stanfordmag.org/contents/stanford-for-all.

56. Olivia Moore, "iTunes U Still Competitive in Online Education," *Stanford Daily*, February 5, 2013, https://stanforddaily.com/2013/02/05/itunes-u-still-competitive-in-online-education/.

57. A. Ng and J. Widom, "Origins of the Modern MOOC (xMOOC)," in *MOOCs: Expectations and Reality: Full Report*, ed. Fiona M. Hollands and Devayani Tirthali (New York: Columbia University, 2014), 34–47.

58. Lou Pugliese, personal communication with the author, March 24, 2022.

Part II: The Business of Higher Education

1. Richard Ohmann and Ira Shor, *Is College Worth It? Class and the Myth of the College Premium* (Baltimore: Johns Hopkins University Press, 2024), 96–97.

2. David A. Bergeron and Carmel Martin, "Strengthening Our Economy through College for All," Center for American Progress, February 19, 2015, https://www.americanprogress.org/article/strengthening-our-economy-through-college-for-all/.

3. Burning Glass Institute and Strada Institute for the Future of Work, "Talent Disrupted: Underemployment, College Graduates, and the Way Forward," 2024, https://www.burningglassinstitute.org/research/underemployment.

4. https://www.bu.edu/questrom/degree-programs/online-mba/; https://giesonline.illinois.edu/explore-programs/online-mba/faqs#; https://omscs.gatech.edu/cost-and-payment-schedule.

5. https://onlinemba.unc.edu/admissions/tuition-financial-aid/; https://dworakpeck.online.usc.edu/msw/program.

6. Census Bureau Releases New Educational Attainment Data, February 24, 2022, press release, https://www.census.gov/newsroom/press-releases/2022/educational-attainment.html#.

7. https://cew.georgetown.edu/cew-reports/the-college-payoff/.

8. Madison Weiss, "The Tortured Path of the Gainful Employment Rule," Center for American Progress, May 17, 2023, https://www.americanprogress.org/article/the-tortured-path-of-the-gainful-employment-rule/.

Chapter 4: Learning Gets Managed and Monetized

1. B. M. Leiner et al., "A Brief History of the Internet," *ACM SIGCOMM Computer Communication Review* 39, no. 5 (2009): 22–31.

2. Ryan Craig, *A New U: Faster + Cheaper Alternatives to College* (Dallas: BenBella Books, 2018).

3. Charlie Eaton, *Bankers in the Ivory Tower: The Troubling Rise of Financiers in US Higher Education* (Chicago: University of Chicago Press, 2022).

4. Andreas Ortman, "Capital Romance," in *Earnings from Learning: The Rise of For-profit Universities*, ed. D. W. Breneman, B. Pusser, and S. E. Turner (Albany: State University of New York Press, 2006).

5. D. J. Deming, C. Goldin, and L. F. Katz, "The For-Profit Postsecondary School Sector: Nimble Critters or Agile Predators?" *Journal of Economic Perspectives* 26, no. 1 (2012): 139–64.

6. A. R. Molnar and B. Sherman, US Office of Education Support of Computer Activities, 1969, https://www.jstor.org/stable/44416808.

7. Ernie Smith, "Microsoft DOS and the Long History of Educational Games," April 28, 2020, *EdTech*, https://edtechmagazine.com/k12/article/2020/04/microsoft-dos-and-long-history-educational-games.

8. Martin Weller, "Twenty Years of Edtech," *Educause Review*, July 2, 2018, https://er.educause.edu/articles/2018/7/twenty-years-of-edtech#fn7.

9. Lou Pugliese, personal communication with the author, March 24, 2022.

10. Scott Jaschik, "Blackboard Patents Challenged," *Inside Higher Ed*, November 30, 2006, https://www.insidehighered.com/news/2006/12/01/blackboard-patents-challenged.

11. David Soo, personal communication with the author, March 18, 2022.

12. https://tech.ed.gov/what-we-do/.

13. https://tech.ed.gov/.

14. Emily Hanford, "The Story of the University of Phoenix," American Public Media, https://americanradioworks.publicradio.org/features/tomorrows-college/phoenix/story-of-university-of-phoenix.html.

15. Taylor Walsh, *Unlocking the Gates: How and Why Leading Universities Are Opening Up Access to Their Courses* (Princeton: Princeton University Press, 2011).

16. Steve Koppes, "University Joins Other Institutions in the Launch of Educational Web Site Fathom," *University of Chicago Chronicle* 19, no. 20 (August 17, 2020), https://chronicle.uchicago.edu/000817/fathom.shtml.

17. Walsh, *Unlocking the Gates*, 31.

18. Robert Tomsho, "Columbia University to Close Fathom.com E-Learning Service," *Wall Street Journal*, January 6, 2003, https://www.wsj.com/articles/SB104188231770411424.

19. Princeton University, Office of Communications, "Oxford, Princeton, Stanford, Yale to Invest $12 Million in Distance Learning Venture," September 28, 2000, https://pr.princeton.edu/news/00/q3/0928-allison.htm.

20. Walsh, *Unlocking the Gates*, 45.

21. Walsh, *Unlocking the Gates*, 53.

22. Charles Vest, "Why MIT Decided to Give Away All Its Course Materials via the Internet," *Chronicle of Higher Education* 50, no. 21 (2004): B20.

23. MIT OpenCourseWare Press Conference, April 4, 2001, https://youtu.be/4XFvqOSRsa8?si=OcUZWh1sZqhXoZ1z

24. MIT OpenCourseWare Press Conference, April 4, 2001.

25. M. Lovett, O. Meyer, and C. Thille, "The Open Learning Initiative: Measuring the Effectiveness of the OLI Statistics Course in Accelerating Student Learning," *Journal of Interactive Media in Education*, no. 1 (2008), https://eric.ed.gov/?id=EJ840810.

26. A. T. Corbett, K. R. Koedinger, and J. R. Anderson, "Intelligent Tutoring Systems," in *Handbook of Human-Computer Interaction*, ed. Martin Helander (Amsterdam: North-Holland, 1997), 849–74.

27. Lovett, Meyer, and Thille, "The Open Learning Initiative."

28. What Works Clearinghouse, "Supporting Postsecondary Success Intervention Report: Open Learning Initiative (OLI)" (Washington, DC: What Works Clearinghouse, 2020).

29. Forum on the Impact of Open Courseware for Higher Education in Developing Countries Final report, https://unesdoc.unesco.org/ark:/48223/pf0000128515.

30. Katie Hafner, "An Open Mind," *New York Times*, April 16, 2010, https://www.nytimes.com/2010/04/18/education/edlife/18open-t.html?smid=url-share.

31. Wenli Li, "The Economics of Student Loan Borrowing and Repayment," *Federal Reserve Bank of Philadelphia Business Review* (third quarter, 2013), https://www.philadelphiafed.org/consumer-finance/education-finance/the-economics-of-student-loan-borrowing-and-repayment.

32. M. Schneider and L. Yin, "The High Cost of Low Graduation Rates: How Much Does Dropping Out of College Really Cost?" *American Institutes for Research* (August 2011), https://eric.ed.gov/?id=ED523102.

33. Jaison R. Abel and Richard Deitz, "Do the Benefits of College Still Outweigh the Costs?" *Current Issues in Economics and Finance* 20, no. 3 (2014), SSRN: https://ssrn.com/abstract=2477864.

34. Bryan Alexander, "Higher Education Reaches an Inflection Point, Continued," May 20, 2013, https://bryanalexander.org/uncategorized/higher-education-reaches-an-inflection-point-continued/.

35. Liat Clark, "Google's Artificial Brain Learns to Find Cat Videos," *Wired*, June 26, 2012, https://www.wired.com/2012/06/google-x-neural-network/.

36. Andrew Ng and Jennifer Widom, "Origins of the Modern MOOC (xMOOC)," in *MOOCs: Expectations and Reality: Full Report*, ed. Fiona M. Hollands and Devayani Tirthali (New York: Columbia University, 2014), 34–47.

37. Theresa Johnston, "Stanford for All," *Stanford Magazine*, September/October 2012, https://stanfordmag.org/contents/stanford-for-all.

38. Amir Efrati, "Start-Up Expands Free Course Offerings Online," *Wall Street Journal*, April 12, 2012, https://www.wsj.com/articles/SB10001424052702303299604577326302609615094.

39. Max Chafkin, "Udacity's Sebastian Thrun, Godfather of Free Online Education, Changes Course," Fast Company, November 14, 2013, https://www.fastcompany.com/3021473/udacity-sebastian-thrun-uphill-climb.

40. A. Anders, "Theories and Applications of Massive Online Open Courses (MOOCs): The Case for Hybrid Design," *International Review of Research in Open and Distributed Learning* 16, no. 6 (2015).

41. Johnston, "Stanford for All."

Chapter 5: MOOCs, 2012

1. Thomas L. Friedman, "Come the Revolution," *New York Times*, May 15, 2012, https://www.nytimes.com/2012/05/16/opinion/friedman-come-the-revolution.html.

2. John Markoff, "Online Education Venture Lures Cash Infusion with 5 Top Universities," *New York Times*, April 18, 2012, https://www.nytimes.com/2012/04/18/technology/coursera-plans-to-announce-university-partners-for-online-classes.html.

3. https://web.stanford.edu/~jurafsky/NLPCourseraSlides.html.

4. Andrew Rice, "Anatomy of a Campus Coup," *New York Times*, September 11, 2012, https://www.nytimes.com/2012/09/16/magazine/teresa-sullivan-uva-ouster.html.

5. Rip Empson, "Online Education Startup Coursera Lands $16M from Kleiner & NEA, Adds John Doerr to Its Board," TechCrunch, April 18, 2012, https://techcrunch.com/2012/04/18/coursera-raises-16m/.

6. https://otl.stanford.edu/about/about-otl.

7. https://facts.stanford.edu/research/innovation/.

8. Marc Sanders, personal communication with the author, September 24, 2021.

9. https://news.stanford.edu/news/2012/september/class2go-online-platform-091212.html.

10. Tamar Lewin, "Harvard and MIT Team Up to Offer Free Online Courses," *New York Times*, May 2, 2012, https://www.nytimes.com/2012/05/03/education/harvard-and-mit-team-up-to-offer-free-online-courses.html.

11. Stanford Faculty Senate, April 19, 2012, 44th Faculty Senate, spring quarter, https://facultysenate.stanford.edu/past-senates/44th-faculty-senate.

12. "Harvard, MIT Launch Online Education Project," *Wall Street Journal*, May 2, 2012, https://www.wsj.com/video/harvard-mit-launch-online-education-project/113E19F2-7324-49B3-A4AD-263C69FCDE39.

13. John Doerr, *Measure What Matters: The Simple Idea That Drives 10x Growth* (London: Penguin UK, 2018).

14. H. Abelson, N. Goodman, and L. Rudolph, Logo Manual, 1974; H. Abelson, "The Creation of OpenCourseWare at MIT," *Journal of Science Education and Technology* 17 (2008): 164–74.

15. Steve Kolowich, "How edX Plans to Earn, and Share, Revenue from Its Free Online Courses," *Chronicle of Higher Education*, February 21, 2013, https://www.chronicle.com/article/how-edx-plans-to-earn-and-share-revenue-from-its-free-online-courses/?cid=gen_sign_in.

16. Jeffrey R. Young, "Elite Colleges Started EdX as a Nonprofit Alternative to Coursera. How Is It Doing?" EdSurge, May 13, 2021, https://www.edsurge.com/news/2021-05-13-elite-colleges-started-edx-as-a-nonprofit-alternative-to-coursera-how-is-it-doing.

17. John Hechinger and Rebecca Buckman, "The Golden Touch of Stanford's President," *Wall Street Journal*, February 24, 2007, https://www.wsj.com/articles/SB117226912853917727.

18. S. W. Leslie and R. H. Kargon, "Selling Silicon Valley: Frederick Terman's Model for Regional Advantage," *Business History Review* 70, no. 4 (1996): 435–72; Annalee Saxenian, *Regional Advantage: Culture and Competition in Silicon Valley and Route 128* (Cambridge, MA: Harvard University Press, 1996).

19. Hechinger and Buckman, "The Golden Touch of Stanford's President."

20. Ry Rivard, "Coursera, edX Continue to Expand," *Inside Higher Ed*, May 21, 2013, https://www.insidehighered.com/quicktakes/2013/05/22/coursera-edx-continue-expand.

21. S. Evans and J. G. Myrick, "How MOOC Instructors View the Pedagogy and Purposes of Massive Open Online Courses," *Distance Education* 36, no. 3 (2015): 295–311.

22. Ken Auletta, "Get Rich U.," New Yorker, April 23, 2012, https://www.newyorker.com/magazine/2012/04/30/get-rich-u.

23. Wenli Li, "The Economics of Student Loan Borrowing and Repayment," *Federal Reserve Bank of Philadelphia Business Review* (third quarter, 2013), https://www.philadelphiafed.org/consumer-finance/education-finance/the-economics-of-student-loan-borrowing-and-repayment.

24. R. B. Archibald and D. H. Feldman, "Explaining Increases in Higher Education Costs," *Journal of Higher Education* 79, no. 3 (2008): 268–95.

25. William G. Bowen, "The 'Cost Disease' in Higher Education: Is Technology the Answer?" Tanner Lectures Stanford University (2012), http://assets.press.princeton.edu/chapters/p10053.pdf.

26. Bowen, "The 'Cost Disease' in Higher Education."

27. W. G. Bowen, *Higher Education in the Digital Age* (Princeton: Princeton University Press, 2015), 63.

28. Jason Orgill and Douglas Hervey, "How Online Innovators Are Disrupting Education," *Harvard Business Review*, November 4, 2011, https://hbr.org/2011/11/how-online-innovators-are-disr.

29. Friedman, "Come the Revolution."

30. https://blog.coursera.org/12-new-universities-join-coursera/.

31. Laura Pappano, "The Year of the MOOC," *New York Times*, November 2, 2012.

32. Roger Riddell, "Coursera Doubles University Partnerships, Pushing Course Count Close to 200," Higher Ed Dive, September 19, 2012, https://www.highereddive.com/news/coursera-doubles-university-partnerships-pushing-course-count-close-to-200/55076/.

33. Charles E. Eesley and William F. Miller, "Impact: Stanford University's Economic Impact via Innovation and Entrepreneurship," *Foundations and Trends® in Entrepreneurship* 14, no. 2 (2018): 130–278.

34. Rob Matheson, "New Report Outlines MIT's Global Entrepreneurial Impact," MIT News, December 9, 2015, https://news.mit.edu/2015/report-entrepreneurial-impact-1209.

35. "Stanford University to Collaborate with edX on Development of Non-profit Open-Source edX Platform," MIT News, April 3, 2013, https://news.mit.edu/2013/stanford-to-collaborate-on-edx-platform-0403.

Chapter 6: Riding the Waves

1. Ry Rivard, "Free to Profit," *Inside Higher Ed*, April 7, 2013, https://www.insidehighered.com/news/2013/04/08/coursera-begins-make-money.

2. E. J. Emanuel, "MOOCs Taken by Educated Few," *Nature* 503, no. 7476 (2013): 342.

3. https://news.wharton.upenn.edu/press-releases/2015/02/wharton-business-foundations-now-available-as-a-specialization-on-coursera/.

4. Dhawal Shah, "Coursera's 2016: Year in Review," *The Report*, December 7, 2016, https://www.classcentral.com/report/coursera-2016-review/.

5. Derek Newton, "Beware of the Great MOOC Bait-and-Switch," *Forbes*, November 19, 2018, https://www.forbes.com/sites/dereknewton/2018/11/19/beware-of-the-great-mooc-bait-and-switch/?sh=258bf12012f2.

6. Varuni Khosla, "Udacity to Focus on Individual Student Projects," *Economic Times*, October 6, 2017, https://economictimes.indiatimes.com/industry/services/education/udacity-to-focus-on-individual-student-projects/articleshow/60963078.cms?from=mdr.

NOTES TO CHAPTER 6   215

7. Shah, "Coursera's 2016: Year in Review."
8. "MOOCs Haven't Lived up to the Hopes and the Hype, Stanford Participants Say," *Stanford Report*, October 15, 2015, https://news.stanford.edu/2015/10/15/moocs-no-panacea-101515/.
9. Dian Schaffhauser, "EdX Begins Testing a Paywall," *Campus Technology*, June 12, 2018, https://campustechnology.com/articles/2018/06/12/edx-begins-testing-a-paywall.aspx.
10. https://blog.coursera.org/welcome-rick-levin-as-ceo-of-coursera/.
11. R. C. Levin, *The Work of the University* (New Haven: Yale University Press, 2008).
12. D. D. Guttenplan, "Out in Front, and Optimistic, about Online Education," *New York Times*, April 14, 2014, https://www.nytimes.com/2014/04/14/education/out-in-front-and-optimistic-about-online-education.html.
13. "The Limits of Open," *Inside Higher Ed*, January 28, 2016, https://www.insidehighered.com/news/2016/01/29/critics-see-mismatch-between-courseras-mission-business-model#.
14. S. Naidu, "The MOOC Is Dead—Long Live MOOC 2.0!" *Distance Education* 41, no. 1 (2020): 1–5.
15. Daphne Koller, "Daphne Koller: 'MOOCs Can Be a Significant Factor in Opening Doors to Opportunity,'" EdSurge, December 31, 2013, https://www.edsurge.com/news/2013-12-31-daphne-koller-moocs-can-be-a-significant-factor-in-opening-doors-to-opportunity.
16. Andrew Maas, Chris Heather, Chuong (Tom) Do, Relly Brandman, Daphne Koller, Andrew Ng, "Ubiquity Symposium: MOOCs and Technology to Advance Learning and Learning Research: Offering Verified Credentials in Massive Open Online Courses," *Ubiquity* (May 2014): 1–11, https://ubiquity.acm.org/article.cfm?id=2591684.
17. Katie Lobosco, "This MBA Costs Less than $22,000," CNN Money, October 20, 2016, https://money.cnn.com/2016/10/20/pf/college/online-mba/.
18. https://blog.coursera.org/announcing-coursera-for-business/.
19. Ry Rivard, "No-Bid MOOCs," *Inside Higher Ed*, July 16, 2013, https://www.insidehighered.com/news/2013/07/17/moocs-spread-quickly-aided-no-bid-deals-public-universities.
20. Marguerite McNeal, "Daphne Koller Bids Farewell to Coursera, Hello to Calico," EdSurge, August 18, 2016, https://www.edsurge.com/news/2016-08-18-daphne-koller-bids-farewell-to-coursera-hello-to-calico.
21. Melissa Korn, "Coursera Names Financial Engines Ex-CEO Jeff Maggioncalda as New Leader," *Wall Street Journal*, June 13, 2017, https://www.wsj.com/articles/coursera-names-financial-engines-ex-ceo-jeff-maggioncalda-as-new-leader-1497365615.

22. Neil Selwyn, "Minding Our Language: Why Education and Technology Is Full of Bullshit . . . and What Might Be Done about It," *Learning, Media and Technology* 41, no. 3 (2016): 437–43, http://doi.org/10.1080/17439884.2015.1012523.

23. Nick Parlante, "Decomposition and Style," 1996, https://cs.stanford.edu/people/nick/compdocs/Decomposition_and_Style.pdf.

24. Carl Straumsheim, "MIT's New Model," *Inside Higher Ed*, October 7, 2015, https://www.insidehighered.com/news/2015/10/08/massachusetts-institute-technology-launch-half-mooc-half-person-masters-degree.

25. I had just joined Wharton after eleven years at Stanford and Stanford professor-founded start-ups (including Coursera) while Price received his PhD from Stanford and understood the culture there.

26. Tressie McMillan Cottom, *Lower Ed: The Troubling Rise of For-Profit Colleges in the New Economy* (New York: New Press, 2017).

27. I moderated this panel and have a copy of this presentation.

28. Jessie Brown and Martin Kurzweil, *The Complex Universe of Alternative Postsecondary Credentials and Pathways* (Cambridge, MA: American Academy of Arts and Sciences, 2017).

29. Lindsay McKenzie, "Arizona State Moves on from Global Freshman Academy," *Inside Higher Ed*, September 16, 2019, https://www.insidehighered.com/digital-learning/article/2019/09/17/arizona-state-changes-course-global-freshman-academy.

30. IBL News, "EdX Creates Its Corporate Solutions Business," iblnews.org, March 8, 2017, https://iblnews.org/edx-creates-corporate-solutions-business/.

31. Settlement Agreement between the United States of America and EdX Inc. under the Americans with Disabilities Act, DJ No. 202-36-255, https://archive.ada.gov/edx_sa.htm.

32. L. T. Hamilton, H. Daniels, C. M. Smith, and C. Eaton, "The Private Side of Public Universities: Third-Party Providers and Platform Capitalism," Centers for Study in Higher Education, 2022, https://escholarship.org/uc/item/7p0114s8.

33. Kevin Carey, "The Creeping Capitalist Takeover of Higher Education," *HuffPost*, April 1, 2019, https://www.huffpost.com/highline/article/capitalist-takeover-college/?src=longreads.

34. C. M. Smith, A. D. Villalobos, L. T. Hamilton, and C. Eaton, "Promising or Predatory? Online Education in Non-Profit and For-Profit Universities," *Social Forces* (2023): soad074.

35. Calculated using the studentaid.gov loan simulator.

36. https://finance.yahoo.com/quote/TWOU/key-statistics.

37. Ben Unglesbee, "2U Emerges from Chapter 11 Bankruptcy," *Higher Ed Dive*, https://www.highereddive.com/news/judge-signs-off-on-2u-bankruptcy-plan/726776/.

38. "Higher Education: Education Needs to Strengthen Its Approach to Monitoring Colleges' Arrangements with Online Program Managers," U.S. GAO, April 5, 2002, https://www.gao.gov/products/gao-22-104463.

39. Lisa Bannon and Andrea Fuller, "USC Pushed a $115,000 Online Degree. Graduates Got Low Salaries, Huge Debts," *Wall Street Journal*, November 19, 2021, https://www.wsj.com/articles/usc-online-social-work-masters-11636435900.

40. Christina Chkarboul, "Former USC Coaches, Parents Implicated in Varsity Blues Scandal Sentenced," *Daily Trojan*, June 29, 2022, https://dailytrojan.com/2022/06/29/former-usc-coaches-parents-implicated-in-varsity-blues-scandal-sentenced/.

41. Adam Elmahrek and Paul Pringle, "Former USC Medical School Dean Used Hard Drugs while Employed at University, Attorney Says," *Los Angeles Times*, May 30, 2018, https://www.latimes.com/local/lanow/la-me-usc-puliafito-medical-board-trial-20180530-story.html.

42. Emma Whitford, "College Endowments Boomed in Fiscal 2021," *Inside Higher Ed*, February 17, 2022, https://www.insidehighered.com/news/2022/02/18/college-endowments-boomed-fiscal-year-2021-study-shows#.

43. Erik Gilbert, "College Finances Are Being Eaten from the Inside," *Chronicle of Higher Education*, November 4, 2021, https://www.chronicle.com/article/college-finances-are-being-eaten-from-the-inside.

44. Margaret Mattes, "The Private Side of Public Education," Century Foundation, August 7, 2017, https://tcf.org/content/report/private-side-public-higher-education/.

45. https://bootcamp.sas.upenn.edu/faq/#1564682338149-501b451b-103e.

46. https://analytics.hbs.edu/.

47. https://www.hbs.edu/about/annualreport/2022/.

48. Sydney Johnson and Tony Wan, "2U's 'Third Chapter' Begins with a $750M Acquisition of Trilogy Education," EdSurge, April 8, 2019, https://www.edsurge.com/news/2019-04-08-2u-s-third-chapter-begins-with-a-750m-acquisition-of-trilogy-education.

49. https://investor.2u.com/news-and-events/press-releases/news-details/2021/2U-Inc.-and-edX-to-Join-Together-in-Industry-Redefining-Combination/default.aspx.

50. K. D. Devkate, S. Warghade, and P. Tilak, "Emerging Trends in Online Educational in India: A Literature Review," *Rabindra Bharati Journal of Philosophy* 23, no. 14 (2022).

51. Manish Singh, "India's Eruditus Valued at $3.2 Billion in $650 Million Fundraise," Tech Crunch, August 11, 2021, https://techcrunch.com/2021/08/11/india-eruditus-valued-at-3-2-billion-in-650-million-fundraise/.

52. https://assets.ey.com/content/dam/ey-sites/ey-com/en_in/topics/education/ey-higher-education-in-india-vision-2047.pdf.

53. Dhawal Shah, "Coursera's 2018: Year in Review," *The Report*, December 10, 2018, https://www.classcentral.com/report/coursera-2018-year-review/.

54. Alex Konrad, "Coursera Fights to Keep the Promise of MOOCs Alive with Corporate Customer Push," *Forbes*, December 20, 2017, https://www.forbes.com/sites/alexkonrad/2017/12/20/coursera-goes-corporate-to-keep-alive-promise-of-moocs/?sh=1bb62eb7543c.

55. Hamilton et al., "The Private Side of Public Universities."

56. F. Hollands and M. Escueta, "How Research Informs Educational Technology Decision-making in Higher Education: The Role of External Research versus Internal Research," *Educational Technology Research and Development* 68 (2020): 163–80.

57. Hamilton et al., "The Private Side of Public Universities."

58. Of twenty-five schools with the largest endowments in 2023, twenty have an online strategy position at the provost office level in 2024. Of these, 85 percent are men, 90 percent have a terminal degree (doctorate, MBA, or JD), and the majority are white.

59. J. Komljenovic, B. Williamson, R. Eynon, and H. C. Davies, "When Public Policy 'Fails' and Venture Capital 'Saves' Education: Edtech Investors as Economic and Political Actors," *Globalisation, Societies and Education* (2023): 1–16.

60. Denise A. Ayo, "On College Campuses, Workplace Inequities Abound," Keough School of Global Affairs, University of Notre Dame, May 3, 2021, https://keough.nd.edu/on-college-campuses-workplace-inequities-abound-dd/.

61. Tess Arena, "Three Key Trends to Watch in the Online Graduate Market," EAB, February 11, 2022, https://eab.com/insights/blogs/adult-learner/key-trends-online-graduate-market/.

62. "The Future of Jobs Report 2018," World Economic Forum, September 17, 2018, https://www.weforum.org/publications/the-future-of-jobs-report-2018/.

63. "Skill Shift: Automation and the Future of the Workforce," McKinsey Global Institute, May 23, 2018, https://www.mckinsey.com/featured-insights/future-of-work/skill-shift-automation-and-the-future-of-the-workforce.

64. Ingrid Lunden, "RPA Startup Automation Anywhere Nabs $300M from SoftBank at a $2.6B Valuation," Tech Crunch, November 15, 2018, https://techcrunch.com/2018/11/15/rpa-startup-automation-anywhere-nabs-300m-from-softbank-at-a-2-6b-valuation/.

65. J. Stine, A. Trumbore, T. Woll, and H. Sambucetti, "Implications of Artificial Intelligence on Business Schools and Lifelong Learning," *Final Report at Academic Leadership Group*, 2019, https://uniconexed.org/research/implications-of-artificial-intelligence-on-business-schools-and-lifelong-learning/.

66. George Siemens, "Learning Analytics: Envisioning a Research Discipline and a Domain of Practice," *Proceedings of the 2nd International Conference on Learning Analytics and Knowledge* (2012): 4–8.

67. R. S. Baker, "Stupid Tutoring Systems, Intelligent Humans," *International Journal of Artificial Intelligence in Education* 26 (2016): 600–614.

Chapter 7: Covid, Cash-Outs, and ChatGPT

1. Lauren Lumpkin, "Court Revives Suits Seeking Refunds after GWU, American Moved Online in Pandemic," *Washington Post*, March 8, 2022, https://www.washingtonpost.com/education/2022/03/08/tuition-lawsuits-george-washington-american-covid/.

2. "Princeton Announces Plan for Fall 2020, Guidelines for Undergraduates Returning to Campus," July 6, 2020, https://www.princeton.edu/news/2020/07/06/princeton-announces-plan-fall-2020-guidelines-undergraduates-returning-campus.

3. https://blog.coursera.org/more-than-1-6-million-learners-around-the-world-benefit-from-partner-contributions-in-courseras-response-to-the-pandemic/.

4. Coursera Keynote from Jeff Maggioncalda, Coursera CEO [2020 Coursera Virtual Conference] https://www.youtube.com/watch?v=hSn8pe_Cai8.

5. V. Leve, "A Rush of Inspiration," *Nature* 612 (2022): S3.

6. National Center for Education Statistics, College Enrollment Rates, *Condition of Education* (U.S. Department of Education, Institute of Education Sciences, 2023), https://nces.ed.gov/programs/coe/indicator/cpb.

7. Katharine Meyer, "The Case for College: Promising Solutions to Reverse College Enrollment Declines," Brookings, June 5, 2023, https://www.brookings.edu/articles/the-case-for-college-promising-solutions-to-reverse-college-enrollment-declines/.

8. https://www.exed.hbs.edu/comprehensive-leadership-programs.

9. Lisa Bannon and Rebecca Smith, "That Fancy University Course? It Might Actually Come from an Education Company," *Wall Street Journal*, July 6, 2022, https://www.wsj.com/articles/that-fancy-university-course-it-might-actually-come-from-an-education-company-11657126489?page=1.

10. L. T. Hamilton, H. Daniels, C. M. Smith, and C. Eaton, "The Private Side of Public Universities: Third-Party Providers and Platform Capitalism," Centers for Study in Higher Education, 2022, https://escholarship.org/uc/item/7p0114s8.

11. https://www.brown.senate.gov/imo/media/doc/01142022_letter_to_opms.pdf.

12. "2U, Inc. and edX Complete Industry-Redefining Combination," November 16, 2021, https://2u.com/latest/2u-inc-and-edx-complete-industry-redefining-combination/.

13. Michael Feldstein, "Is the edX Acquisition a Big Deal?" eLiterate, June 30, 2021, https://eliterate.us/is-the-edx-acquisition-a-big-deal/.

14. "2U, Inc. and edX Complete Industry-Redefining Combination," November 16, 2021, https://2u.com/latest/2u-inc-and-edx-complete-industry-redefining-combination/.

15. John S. Rosenberg and Jonathan Shaw, "EdX Exit," *Harvard Magazine*, September/October 2021, https://www.harvardmagazine.com/2021/08/jhj-edx-sold#.

16. Phil Hill, "Additional Points on 2U's Acquisition of edX," *On EdTech Newsletter*, November 17, 2021, https://onedtech.philhillaa.com/p/additional-points-on-2us-acquisition-of-edx.

17. Riley de León, "Coursera Closes up 36%, Topping $5.9 Billion Market Cap in Wall Street Debut," CNBC, March 31, 2021, https://www.cnbc.com/2021/03/31/coursera-ipo-cour-begins-trading-on-the-nyse.html.

18. www.coursera.org/courseraplus.

19. OECD (2024), Income inequality (indicator), https://doi.org/10.1787/459aa7f1-en.

20. Becky Ham, "Daphne Koller: Online Learning Is Transforming Careers Worldwide," American Association for the Advancement of Science, February 14, 2015, https://www.aaas.org/news/daphne-koller-online-learning-transforming-careers-worldwide.

21. A. Trumbore, "Learner Behavior and Career Benefits in Business Massive Open Online Courses," in *Proceedings of the 15th International Conference of the Learning Sciences-ICLS 2021*, ed. E. de Vries, Y. Hod, and J. Ahn (Bochum: International Society of the Learning Sciences, 2021), 935–36.

22. Susan D'Agostino, "As Microcredentials Boom, Employers' Hiring Platforms Fumble," *Inside Higher Ed*, March 27, 2023, https://www.insidehighered.com/news/2023/03/28/microcredentials-boom-employers-hiring-platforms-fumble.

23. Ingrid Lunden, "Google and Coursera Launch Program to Train More IT Support Specialists," Tech Crunch, January 16, 2018, https://techcrunch.com/2018/01/16/google-and-coursera-launch-program-to-train-more-it-support-specialists/.

24. https://grow.google/certificates/it-support/.

25. Lisa Gevelber, "Preparing Learners for Growing Industries with Higher Ed," October 13, 2022, https://blog.google/outreach-initiatives/grow-with-google/industry-specializations/.

26. https://investor.coursera.com/news/news-details/2023/Coursera-Reports-Second-Quarter-2023-Financial-Results/default.aspx.

27. https://www.nsf.gov/awardsearch/advancedSearchResult?ProgEleCode=132Y&BooleanElement=Any&BooleanRef=Any&ActiveAwards=true.

28. https://www.holoniq.com/notes/2019-artificial-intelligence-global-education-report.

29. "Reskilling in the Age of AI," *Harvard Business Review*, September/October 2023, https://hbr.org/2023/09/reskilling-in-the-age-of-ai.

30. https://openai.com/blog/chatgpt.

31. "ChatGPT Mania May Be Cooling, but a Serious New Industry Is Taking Shape," *Economist*, September 21, 2023, https://www.economist.com/leaders/2023/09/21/chatgpt-mania-may-be-cooling-but-a-serious-new-industry-is-taking-shape.

32. Debby R. E. Cotton, Peter A. Cotton, and J. Reuben Shipway, "Chatting and Cheating: Ensuring Academic Integrity in the Era of ChatGPT," *Innovations in Education and Teaching International* 61, no. 2 (2024): 228–39; M. A. Cardona, R. J. Rodríguez, and K. Ishmael, "Artificial Intelligence and the Future of Teaching and Learning: Insights and Recommendations," 2023, https://policycommons.net/artifacts/3854312/ai-report/4660267/.

33. https://teaching.cornell.edu/generative-artificial-intelligence.

34. https://www.nsf.gov/cise/ai.jsp.

35. https://finance.yahoo.com/quote/COUR?p=COUR&.tsrc=fin-srch; "Coursera to Raise about $519 Million in U.S. IPO at over $4 Billion Valuation," Reuters, March 30, 2021, https://www.reuters.com/article/us-coursera-ipo/coursera-to-raise-about-519-million-in-u-s-ipo-at-over-4-billion-valuation-idUSKBN2BN05R/.

36. https://www.holoniq.com/notes/edtech-vc-collapse-at-580m-for-q1-not-even-an-ai-tailwind-could-hold-up-the-10-year-low?ref=newsletters.holoniq.com.

37. Rod Berger, "Blackboard's Founder Breaking New Ground with Class Technologies," *Forbes*, June 17, 2022, https://www.forbes.com/sites/rodberger/2022/06/17/blackboards-founder-breaking-new-ground-with-class-technologies/?sh=52f5259c5ee3.

38. Daphne Koller, personal correspondence with the author, August 9, 2020.

39. Ingrid Lunden, "Engageli Nabs $33M More for Its Collaborative Video-Based Teaching Platform," Tech Crunch, May 11, 2021, https://techcrunch.com/2021/05/11/engageli-nabs-33m-more-for-its-collaborative-video-based-teaching-platform/.

40. https://www.coursera.org/business/resources/webinar/coursera-conference-2023-jeff-keynote.

Conclusion

1. Charlie Eaton and Mitchell L. Stevens, "Universities as Peculiar Organizations," *Sociology Compass* 14, no. 3 (2020): e12768.

2. Douglas Belkin, "Americans Are Losing Faith in College Education, WSJ-NORC Poll Finds," *Wall Street Journal*, March 31, 2023, https://www.wsj.com

/articles/americans-are-losing-faith-in-college-education-wsj-norc-poll-finds-3a836ce1.

3. Steven Levy, *Hackers: Heroes of the Computer Revolution* (Vol. 14) (Garden City, NY: Anchor Press/Doubleday, 1984).

4. H. A. Giroux, *The Violence of Organized Forgetting: Thinking beyond America's Disimagination Machine* (San Francisco: City Lights Publishers, 2014), 136.

INDEX

Note: Page numbers in italics indicate figures

Ackerman, Edith, 41
Advanced Research Projects Agency (ARPA), 18, 33
Advanced Research Projects Agency Network (ARPANET), 33
"Advances in Computer-Based Education" (Bitzer and Alpert), 52, 55
Africa, 164
Agarwal, Anant, 120, 128, 140, 145–48, 183
Allison Jr., Herbert M., 103
All Learn, 102–3
Alpert, Daniel, 47, 50
Ames, Morgan, 79–80
andragogy, 111
Apollo, 101. *See also* University of Phoenix
Apple, 75
Arizona State University, 148
Arkansas State University, 152–53
ARPANET, 94
"Artificial Intelligence: A General Survey" (Lighthill), 59–60
Artificial Intelligence Laboratory (AIL), 37–38
Atkinson, Richard, 44, 46, 62

automatic tutor: Brentwood Elementary School and, 15–17; Suppes and, 44–45, 63
Automation Anywhere, 163
Avida, Dan, 179–80

"Baby in a Box," 23–24
Baker, Ryan, 164
Berners-Lee, Tim, 94
beta testing, 26
Bitzer, Don: AI and, 176; biography of, 19, 67; creative funding and, 54; plasma displays and, 51; PLATO and, 2–3, 33; PLATO I and, 47–48, *48*; PLATO III, 49–50; PLATO IV and, 50–53, 67–73; relationship with Suppes and Papert and, 54–56
Blackboard, 98–99. *See also* learning management systems (LMSs)
Bloom, Benjamin, 7
Botton, Leo, 60
Bowen, William G., 129–32
Brentwood Elementary School, 15–17
Brown, Sherrod, 168

Carnegie Corporation, 44
Carnegie Learning, 106

Carnegie Mellon, 106–7
Carr, William, 29
Center for American Progress, 88
certificate programs, 139–41, 154–55, 159, 167, 174. *See also* higher education
Charles River Ventures, 111
Chasen, Michael, 98, 179–81
Chat-GPT, 175
child psychology, 41
children's education: the automatic tutor and, 15–17; CAI Experiments and, 44–46; EPGY and, 81–83; OLPC and, 78–80; Papert and, 20–22, 33–34; Project MAC and, 39; technology and, 2. *See also* Papert, Seymour
China, 164
Christensen, Clayton, 131–32
Class, 179–82
Class2Go, 119–20
classrooms, 41–42
the Cold War, 4
"College for All," 88
Columbia University, 101–2
commercialization: of the college degree, 58–59; of software, 57–58
computer assisted instruction (CAI), 32–33; IMSSS and, 63; NRMP and, 65–67; Papert on, 55. *See also* Bitzer, Don; Papert, Seymour; PLATO; Suppes, Patrick
Computer-based Education Research Laboratory (CERL), 51–53
Computer Curriculum Corporation, 46, 54, 57, 61–62, 64–65
computers: children's education and, 2; connectivity and, 132; in education, 4, 17, 19, 31–33, 42, 44–45, 47, 55, 73–74, 97; NovaNET and, 72; Papert and, 20, 54, 77–78; PDP-1 and, 38–39; Suppes and, 81, 85. *See also* IBM; PLATO
The Conference on the Art and Science of the Automatic Teaching of Verbal and Symbolic Skills, 26–29
constructionism, 41, 75–76
constructivism, 41
Control Data Corporation (CDC), 50–51, 54, 58, 67–73
cost disease, 129–32
Coursera: business to business and, 143–44; certificate programs and, 139–41, 157, 159; code ownership and, 113–14; competition and, 119–20; Covid-19 pandemic and, 166; criticism of, 140, 142; Doerr and, 123–24; entry level role certificates and, 174–75; founders and, 110–12; growth of, 119, 132–34, 136, 166; history of online education and, 5–6; IPO and, 166, 172–73, 177; Levin and, 141–42; new lines of business and, 143; online degrees and, 143, 158–59; origin story of, 120–22; peer-review functionality and, 124; performance optimization and, 135–36; platform instability and, 115–17, 124, 132–34, 142; pricing model and, 143–44; Stanford Office of Technology Licensing and, 117–20; team photo (2012) and, 125; understaffing and, 133. *See also* higher education; Massive Open Online Courses (MOOCs); Stanford University
courseware. *See* learning management systems (LMSs)

INDEX 225

Covid-19 pandemic, 3, 165–68
credentials, *167*
Crow, Michael, 101–2

Dear, Brian, 67, 72
debugging, 76
Demara, Ashwin, 157–58
"Dial a Drill," 64–65
digital speech, 45, 63
Disrupting Class: How Disruptive Innovation Will Change the Way the World Learns (Christensen), 131
disruption: Coursera and, 6; educational technology and, 1–2; Khan Academy and, 7–8; MOOCs and, 131–33. *See also* Coursera; educational technology; edX
Doerr, John, 123–24
Dragas, Helen, 117
Duckworth, Angela, 76
Duke University, 166

Eaton, Charlie, 183
educational entrepreneurs, 3, 8, 67–73, 94, 190, 197
educational technology: AI and, 175; collective forgetting and, 6–7, 17, 189–91; distance learning and, 43, 61, 102; early experiments with, 2–3; the future of, 176–82; history of, 17–21; homogeneity of decision makers and, 178–79; how universities select technology and, 8; market size and, 17, 156–58; the OET and, 99–100; QWERTY phenomenon and, 34–36; venture capital funding and, *89*, 90–91. *See also* computer assisted instruction (CAI); Coursera; edX; higher education;

learning management systems (LMSs); Massive Open Online Courses (MOOCs); Stanford Instructional Television Network (SITN)
Education Program for Gifted Youth (EPGY), 81–83, 85
edX: acquisition of, 166, 169–72; Covid-19 pandemic and, 166; founding of, 119–20; growth of, 128; MicroMasters and, 145–49; OLPC initiative and, 80; platform stability and, 140; positioning of, 124–25, 141; unbundling and, 145–46 (*See also* Massachusetts Institute of Technology (MIT)). *See also* Harvard University; higher education; Masssachusetts Institute of Technology (MIT); Massive Open Online Courses (MOOCs)
Emeritus, 157–58
Engageli, 179–82
Eruditus, 158
Etchemendy, John, 121–22

Fathom, 101–2
Feldstein, Michael, 170
flipping the classroom, 112
for-profit universities: the college degree as an investment and, 58–59; growth of, 96–97; the internet and, 96–97; student loans and, 3, 94. *See also* student loans; University of Phoenix
Fortune, Ron, 62
Friedman, Thomas, 113, 132–33
funding: AI Winter and, 57, 59–60; automatic tutor and, 15–17; computer assisted instruction and, 32–34; government, 4, 31–34,

funding (*continued*)
53–56; Military Authorization Act, 53; National Defense Education Act (NDEA) and, 17–18, 31–32; PLATO IV and, 50; for universities, 58
"The Future of Academic Credentials" (panel), 147

Galanter, Eugene, 26–28
Gallie, Thomas, 32, 52
generative AI: Advanced Research Projects Agency (ARPA) and, 18; AI Winter and, 57, 59–60; Covid-19 pandemic and, 175; Khan Academy and, 7; NSF funding and, 176; Papert and, 3, 37–38; personalization and, 176; practical problem solving and, 59–60; as a threat to universities and, 163
GetSmarter, 155
Gilbert, Erik, 152–53
Goldberg, Adele, 55
Google, 110, 174
grit, 76

Harvard University, 119–20, 155, 169–71, 189. *See also* edX; higher education
Hennessy, John, 122–23, 126–29
higher education: AI as a threat to teaching and, 163; AI use by universities and, 163–64; certificate programs and, 91, 139–41, 155, 159; clash between hacker ethic and university culture and, 187–88; commercialization of the internet and, 94–95; cost disease of, 129–32; Covid-19 pandemic and, 3, 165–68; credentials and, *167*; customer acquisition costs and, 168; definition of a university, 183; demands for, 94–96; financialization of, 3, 10, 87–91; for-profit universities and, 3, 88; the future of edtech and, 176–79; hierarchy in, 185–86; importance of, 109; increase in degree programs and, 88, 90; learning analytics centers and, 164; learning centers and, 164; LMSs and, 97–99, 179–82; market for, *171*; need for reform and, 10–11, 185–86; online degrees and, 158–59; as a poorly run business, 186–87; response to edtech and, 183; revenue streams and, 167–68; ROI and, 87; stacking and, 145–49, 159; technology selection by universities and, 8; tuition increases and, 87, 188–89; unbundling and, 145–49, 188; universities being taken advantage of and, 160–62; university hierarchies and, 162; use of tuition dollars for OPMs and, 149–50, 168–69. *See also* Coursera; Massive Open Online Courses (MOOCs)
Higher Education Act (HEA), 95
Hill, Phil, 172
Hurd, Cuthbert, 26

IBM: PLATO IV and, 50–51; Suppes funding and, 57; teaching machines and, 24–25, 25, 26, 28–29
"The Ideal Teacher" (Galanter), 26–27
India, 156–58
"Information Technology and Education: Computer Criticism *vs.* Technocentric Thinking" (Papert), 76–77
inquiry teaching logics, 49

Institute for Mathematical Studies in the Social Sciences (IMSSS), 44–46, 63–64
Interactive Radio Instruction (IRI), 66
the internet, 4, 93–94, 96–97

Katzman, John, 150–51
Khan, Sal, 6–8
Khan Academy, 6–8, 66
Kindel, Alexander, 3
Kleiner Perkins (KP), 123, 128
Koedingeer, Ken, 106
Koller, Daphne, 112–13, 119, 122, 128, 133–34, 143–44, 148, 179–81. *See also* Coursera

Lamar University, 153
learners, 173–75
learning centers, 164
learning management systems (LMSs), 83, 85–86, 97–99, 179–82
Lego, 58. *See also* Logo (programming language)
Lego Mindstorms, 73
Levin, Rick, 103, 141, 143–44
Licklider, J.C.R., 93–94
Lighthill, James, 59–60
Logo (programming language), 20, 42, 58, 74–76, 78
Logo Computer Systems, Inc. (LCSI), 73–75

machine learning, 39–40
Maggioncalda, Jeff, 158, 166, 181–82
Mansfield, Mike, 53
Massive Open Online Courses (MOOCs): adoption of, 128–35; Andrew Ng and, 111; BRICs countries and, 156–58; certificate programs and, 139–41;
commercialization of the college degree and, 58; condemnation of, 140; course completion rates and, 142; Covid-19 pandemic and, 165–68; credentials and, *167*; digital education market size and, 171, *171*; disruption and, 131–33; NRMP and, 66; OLPC initiative and, 80; PLATO I and, 47–48, *48*; stacking and, 145–49; Stanford and, 9–10; unbundling and, 145–49, 183, 188. *See also* Coursera; edX
McCarthy, John, 44–45
MicroMasters, 145–46, 148. *See also* edX
Military Authorization Act, 53
Mindstorms (Papert), 20, 42, 75–76
Minsky, Marvin, 20, 33–34, 38–39, 59
Massachusetts Institute of Technology (MIT): educational entrepreneurship and, 60; edX and, 119–20, 124, 126–28, 136–38, 140, 145, 148, 169–71, 189; hacker culture and, 74, 77–78, 187; Medial Lab, 74, 77–78, 105; MITx and, 120; OpenCourseWare and, 104–5; Open edX Initiative and, 137–38. *See also* higher education
Mitchell, John, 85, 110
Mitros, Piotr, 119–20
Molnar, Andrew, 32–33, 54, 97

National Computer Systems, 72
National Defense Education Act (NDEA), 17–18, 31–32. *See also* funding
National Science Foundation, 54, 69–70, 81, 175–76
national security, 31

Negroponte, Nicholas, 78–80
Ng, Andrew, 110–12, 122, 124, 128, 133–34, 141, 148. *See also* Coursera
Nicaragua, 65–67
Nicaragua Radio Mathematics Project (NRMP), 65–67
Norris, Bill, 50, 72
Norvig, Peter, 133
NovaNET, 72–73
NovoEd, 118

Office of Educational Technology (OET), 99–100
O'Mara, Margaret, 2
One Laptop Per Child initiative, 20, 78–80
Online High School, 81, 83–85
Online Program Managers (OPMs): Arkansas State University and, 152–53; edX acquisition and, 169–70; Harvard and, 155; Lamar University and, 153; noncredit learners and, 154; university partnerships and, 150–56, 159–60, 168–69; USC and, 152; use of tuition dollars and, 149–50, 168–69
Open AI, 175
OpenCourseWare, 104–5
Open Educational Resources (OER), 80, 86, 107–8
Open Learning Initiative (OLI), 106–7
Open University in the United Kingdom, 107–8
O'Shea, Tim, 76

Papert, Seymour: AI and, 37–38, 59, 176; ARPA funding and, 33–34; Artificial Intelligence Laboratory (AIL) and, 38–39; biography of, 20; the classroom as an inefficient learning environment and, 41–42; constructionism and, 41, 75–76; criticism of educational research practices and, 76–77; debugging and, 76; early life of, 40; hacker culture and, 77–78; and the ignoring of his ideas, 73–74, 77; influence of, 39–40; Logo and, 2, 20, 42, 74; MIT Media Lab and, 77–78; OLPC initiative and, 78–80; QWERTY phenomenon and, 34–36; relationship with Bitzer and Suppes and, 54–56; the student programs the computer and, 34, 40, 75; views on teachers and, 74; work at MIT and, 73
Paucek, Chip, 149
"pay if you pass" model, 148
Pea, Roy, 76
Pearson, 72–73
Perceptrons (Papert and Misnky), 20, 59–60
Pettit, Joseph M., 61
Piaget, Jean, 41
Pittinsky, Matthew, 98
plasma displays, 51, 72
PLATO: additional developments and, 69–70; CERL and, 51–52; creation of, 2–3; PLATO I, 47–48, 48; PLATO II, 49; PLATO III, 49–50; PLATO IV, 50–53, 58, 67–73, 68
Pressey, Sidney, 21–22, 24
Price, Vince, 146–47
Princeton University, 102–3, 166
Pugliese, Lou, 86, 98

QWERTY phenomenon, 34–36

Reif, Rafael, 120

Science Research Council, 60
Scratch (programming language), 20
Silicon Valley, 2
Simon and Schuster, 62
Skinner, B. F., 23–24
Slottow, H. G., 51
social media, 132
The Society of Mind (Minsky), 39
soft launch, 26
Solomon, Cynthia, 39, 75
Stanford University: All Learn and, 102–3; Class2Go and, 119–20; Coursera's code and, 117–20; Coursera's origin and, 120–22; entrepreneurial approach of, 33, 46, 60, 67, 189; EPGY and, 81–83, 85; Hennessy and, 126–28; Massive Open Online Courses (MOOCs) and, 9–10; Office of Technology Licensing and, 117–20, 126–27; online education experiments and, 85; Online High School and, 81, 83–85; Open edX Initiative and, 137–38; Stanford Instructional Television Network (SITN) and, 9, 61, 127. *See also* Coursera; higher education
Stanford Artificial Intelligence Library (SAIL), 45
Stanford Center for Professional Development (SCPD), 61
Stanford Instructional Television Network (SITN), 9, 61
Stevens, Mitchell, 3, 147–48, 183
student loans: advertising spending and, 168–69; commercialization of the college degree and, 58–59; compared to other household debt, 109; federal oversight and, 155, 171–72; for-profit universities and, 3, 88; government limits on, 94; HEA reauthorization and, 95–96; outstanding debt and, 88, 129; privatization of, 87–88
Sullivan, Theresa, 117
Suppes, Patrick: AI and, 176; automatic tutor and, 44–45, 63; biography of, 19; CCC and, 61–62; computer assisted instruction and, 5; Computer Curriculum Corporation and, 46, 57; creative funding and, 54; digital speech and, 63; distance learning and, 43; early life of, 43; EPGY and, 81–83; funding and, 33, 57; IMSSS and, 44–45, 63; "individual Aristotle" and, 2–3; neuroscience and, 85; Nicaragua Radio Mathematics Project (NRMP) and, 65–67; Online High School, 81, 83–85; relationship with Papert and Bitzer, 54–56; success of, 67

teaching machines: air crib and, 23–24; Automatic Teacher machine and, 21–22; Carr and, 29; Galanter and, 26–28; IBM and, 24–25, 25, 26, 28–29; PLATO and, 47–48, 48; PLATO III and, 49–50; PLATO IV and, 50–53, 67–73; as a waste of the potential of computers, 42. *See also* educational technology
technology executives, 2
Terman, Fred, 45, 127
Texas Instruments, 74–75
Thrun, Sebastian, 110–11, 120
Tough, Paul, 10
Trilogy Bootcamps, 154–55
Trumbore, Anne M., 4–5, 84, 125, 136
Turtles. *See* Logo (programming language)
TUTOR. *See* PLATO

"20 Things to Do with a Computer" (Papert), 55
2U, 150–52, 154–55, 169–71, *171*, 172. See also edX; Online Program Managers (OPMs)
two-sigma effect, 7

Udacity, 140
UNESCO, 107–8
University of Illinois: CDC and, 69–72; Coursera and, 143; educational entrepreneurship and, 60; NovaNET and, 72–73; PLATO and, 33, 51–53. See also Bitzer, Don; PLATO
University of Oxford, 102–3
University of Pennsylvania, 139, 154
University of Phoenix, 100–101. See also for-profit universities
University of Southern California (USC), 152
University of Virginia, 117
U.S. Agency for International Development (USAID), 65–67
"The Uses of Computers in Education" (Suppes), 45, 55
"U.S. Office of Education Support of Computer Activities," 97

venture capital, 2, 177, 189
Vest, Charles, 104–5

Warren, Elizabeth, 168
Warschauer, Mark, 80
Wei, Pang, 114
Western Cooperative for Educational Telecommunications (WCET), 107–8
Wharton School, 139–40, 144, 147, 157–58
Widom, Jennifer, 110
William and Flora Hewlett Foundation, 107–8
World Wide Web, 94. See also the internet

Yale University, 102–3
Yue, Dick, 104